REMEMBERING BRAD

REMEMBERING BRAD:

ON THE LOSS OF A SON TO AIDS

H. WAYNE SCHOW

With Journal
Entries by
Brad Schow

Signature Books   Salt Lake City   1995

Dust jacket and frontispiece photo: Brad in New York, 1979
Dust jacket design: Clarkson Creative

"Epilogue: The Great Western Cooperative" first appeared in *Weber Studies* 10 (Fall 1993), 3.

99   98   97   96   95   6   5   4   3   2   1

Library of Congress Cataloging-in-Publication Data
    Remembering Brad : on the loss of a son to AIDS / by H. Wayne Schow ; with journal entries by Brad Schow.
        p.   cm.
ISBN 1-56085-070-1
1. Schow, Brad—Health. 2. AIDS (Disease)—Patients—United States—Idaho—Biography. 3. Mormon gays—United States—Idaho—Biography. I. Schow, Brad. II. Title.
RC607.A26S3739 1995
362.1'969792'0092—dc20
    [B]   94-4031
                                                    CIP

For Sandra

who walked this road with me.

Contents

Prologue

The mind is an instrument for arranging the
world in accordance with its own needs and desires.
[Hence] its arrangements must be fictive.
—Frank Kermode

It's a long way from New York or Los Angeles to Pocatello, Idaho.
The distance is not measured simply in miles. Here in this provincial
place, in the mountains on the edge of the Snake River Plain, life
seems less pressured, less complicated.

The distance—and difference—is partly a matter of pace. We
don't really have a fast lane in Pocatello. What doesn't happen today
can wait for tomorrow. And the distance is partly a matter of elbow
room. There aren't so many of us compressed together here.
Perhaps that is why our crime rates are low, racial tensions are
barely discernible, and you can walk clean streets in any part of
town safely, day or night. When you do feel the urge to get out of
town, scenic Idaho is immediately all around you, open and
accessible. The sun shines brightly, the air is clear, and you can see
the Lost River Range rising above the desert seventy miles away.

Our distance from the cosmopolitan places is partly too a matter
of style. We don't set trends here, we don't dictate fashion. You
don't see evidence of great wealth. We're probably not on the
cutting edge of anything. Our style and values are more those of

middle America. Most of us know and like our neighbors; most of us live conventionally, predictably; most of us avoid tension-producing extremes.

For these reasons, Pocatello is a comfortable place. Here you feel largely sheltered from the ills that beset contemporary urban life. Here you generally expect life to be kind.

In this sunny environment, where he had grown to manhood, my oldest son Brad died of AIDS. That was not kind. Somehow it still seems to me, eight years later, not the sort of thing that should have happened in southern Idaho. The cultural geography is altogether wrong.

That sounds terribly naive, I know. For, of course, taboo sexual orientation and taboo illness and untimely death occur everywhere, including sheltered uncosmopolitan places. But they aren't always acknowledged. Somehow we pretend they aren't there. My story of the brief life of a gay son and the response of his Pocatello family is different in some respects from what it would have been had it occurred in New York or San Francisco, for it takes place in a conservatively backlit context of denial.

And that is precisely why I think this story should be told. Though it seems anomalous—the wrong events in the wrong place—I know now what I did not know eight years ago, that this is a common story, lived by other homosexuals and their families in middle American places like Pocatello, a story unfortunately suppressed because of culturally induced shame and fear. As a result, those who dare not express their pain in the face of society's intolerance suffer in closeted silence, and the world goes on thinking that such things occur only in the far off environments of New York and San Francisco.

This book is about Brad, whose temperamental complexity stretched the scenarios normally planned for young Mormons. In writing about him, and by that means attempting to understand his complexity, I have come to realize that this book is also about me, and about the process of sorting things out. The years continue to pass, yet I cannot be done with thinking of him and the impact of his life on mine. In a manner I would never have predicted, he became and continues to be my teacher. That is a paradox worth exploring.

The miscellany that is collected here evolved piecemeal, without initially any intent of its being made into a book. I lost a son in 1986, and I had to try to make sense out of that absurdity. I wrote for therapeutic reasons. Over a period of several years I took up new facets of this involved narrative as the necessary perspectives dawned on me, without giving much thought as I went along to what I had written earlier.

My first response was a long letter to a Mormon apostle in early 1987, subsequently revised and published as an essay in *Sunstone* magazine in February 1990 and reprinted in *Peculiar People: Mormons and Same-Sex Orientation* the next year. Written shortly after Brad's death, it grew out of my conviction at the time that matters need not have turned out for him as they did. If external conditions had been otherwise, if the theological, institutional, and social causes of his impasse could have been identified and "fixed," then he would not have needed to suffer. That first piece of writing was a reflex action on my part, in retrospect noteworthy for its good intentions and naivete.

A year or so later, as my hope for external fixes waned, a lamentation (the first essay in this collection) emerged from a more fully acknowledged existential mood. The essay on grief followed, and about that time I realized that if my intent was to present Brad's story to others, he could tell parts of it far more insightfully than I. Hence, the decision to incorporate selections from his journals. Having by this time come at these events from several perspectives, I recognized that Brad's life could be seen as a search for a spiritual standing place—and that, in a less dramatic way, was true of my life as well. The personal ambivalence I felt pursuing that search within a spiritual community, and that I am sure Brad felt even more intensely, found allegorical expression in "The Great Western Cooperative," included here as an epilogue.

There is some degree of repetition in these selections. I hope the reader will understand it to result from my compelling need to sift and resift these experiences in order to puzzle out their nuances. And corollary thereto, such repetitions reveal that the book as a whole has not an entirely consistent point of view, since my attitudes changed as time passed. The man who wrote the letter in 1987 is not the same one who a year later wrote the essay on tragedy. And so on. The same is true of Brad's journal entries, which are shot through with contradictions. I have not attempted to remove these inconsistencies, for they illustrate the complex and problematic reality of my life, and of Brad's, during this period, indeed of human lives generally.

Experiences of the kind treated here are not permanently fixed as they occur. The meanings will not hold still because we cannot (or will not) hold still in response to them. Not only do new, subsequent experiences change us from what we were, the past itself changes as well because, ourselves altered, we see it differently. Its truth cannot be detached from our perception. In our continuing assessment of it, we attach additional significance to some features and de-emphasize the significance of others. In this way I have come to realize that we create our own fictions, which is an important outcome for me in the sorting-out process this book describes.

I. On Tragedy and the Death of a Son
[July 1988]

So quick bright things come to confusion.
—*A Midsummer Night's Dream*

In common speech the word "tragedy" has become roughly synonymous with personal misfortune, especially if life is lost. A father of a young family is killed in an automobile accident, a beautiful child dies of a blood disease, an airliner smashes into a mountain carrying a hundred people to their deaths: such occurrences are pronounced tragedies, especially by those who knew the victims.

But in a stricter sense the tragic vision of life embodies more than simply misfortune and loss, more than victimization and pathos. Works such as Sophocles' *Oedipus the King*, Shakespeare's *Othello*, and Goethe's *Faust* impress on us a paradox, that tragedy has a powerful affirmative side. Misfortune notwithstanding, tragic vision ultimately makes us aware of impressive dimensions in human nature. Instead of plunging us into despair at the prospect of life's cruel uncertainties, tragedy in the strict sense reconciles us to existence because it makes us believe that we can be greater than our fall.

The essence of tragedy may be understood by examining the

nature of the world in which it happens and the nature of the individual who is centrally involved. The protagonist's downfall occurs in part because he is subject to powerful external forces inimical to his needs and desires. Or, as one critic expresses it, "tragedy explores thwarted energy and possibility."

Yet the catastrophe that overwhelms the central figure is seldom simply a matter of externalities impinging on his life. Aristotle wrote that such a one is not perfect but has a "flaw." Accordingly, he bears some responsibility for his fall. For example, his impasse may derive from powerful internal contradictions. Or his flaw may be just that he refuses to accommodate external demands. Although by conforming to them he might well avoid catastrophe, he refuses to compromise. Where most of us would retreat from confrontation, his flaw may be just that he insists on his dignity, his pride, his sense of what he justly desires though it means that he must suffer ruin as a consequence.

In the process of a losing confrontation with overwhelming forces, the tragic figure achieves impressive stature, a stance that compels admiration. It may be manifest in courage, tenacity, or integrity, in philosophical insight or moral vision. However it is revealed, we know we are in the presence of someone extraordinary. For this reason, in an age when the word "hero" makes us uncomfortable, we nevertheless accept the logically-consistent phrase "tragic hero." Ultimately, tragedy may not clarify the great enigmas or diminish the uncertainties of life, but it assures us there are some of our kind whose existential response to those terrible dilemmas can be awe-inspiring.

It follows that tragedy cannot occur instantly, in a vacuum. It requires a context of choice and response, an opportunity for human stature to develop in the face of extreme opposition. Life-taking accidents, so often casually misnamed as tragic, mostly lack such context.

I review here these commonplaces concerning tragedy because they seem particularly relevant to events I have recently witnessed. I rehearse them because their humanistic perspective helps me find affirmative dimension in a matter otherwise simply devastating. The matter which provokes these reflections is the death of my oldest son, Brad, on December 5, 1986, from AIDS.

It is not easy to lose a son. Francis Bacon observed that when we marry and have children, we give hostages to fortune. Few people really know this when they set up in the business of parenting. In our time, we expect our children to outlive us. We expect them to realize the potential of a full life. We expect them to go farther, to be happier than we. And so whatever the cause of an early death, no parent finds it easy to reconcile. Among the losses that humans sustain, this surely is one of the most significant. Yet that in itself does not make such loss tragic.

Brad was twenty-eight years old at the time of his death. After high school, he spent two years at university studies (in Pocatello and Salt Lake City), dropped out to move to Los Angeles, and returned after four years to continue work in Logan, Utah, toward a degree. At the end of his second year at Utah State University, he came home to Pocatello for the summer to help us construct a new residence. But the AIDS virus had begun its deadly work, and so it was not carpentry but confrontation with disease that would engage him immediately and for the remaining year and a half of his life.

On the surface these facts do not allow us to call Brad's experience tragic, for they tell us nothing about the contexts that evoked choice and action, without which the question of tragedy is moot. I want now to write about those contexts. I want now to trace the complex threads of his life, to remember how he responded as that complicated fabric was being woven.

Among the forces that shaped Brad's life, two stand out prominently. First, he was born to Mormon parents who reared him strictly according to the moral vision of that religion. Second, he was born homosexual. To understand his choices and their outcome, one must understand how these forces came into conflict and ultimately how for him in his standing place they were irreconcilable.

Brad's Mormon roots on both sides of the family go back well over a century. Up until 1950 virtually all members of the extended family branches lived in Utah and Idaho. All of Brad's aunts and uncles and their spouses, all of his great-aunts and -uncles and their spouses (save one), and all of his grandparents and great grandparents were members of the faith. Even today there are no more than a handful of non-Mormons in the extended families.

My wife Sandra and I grew up in orthodox Mormon homes in a southern Idaho town where 85 percent of the population was Mormon. We went to church regularly, participating in a religious community whose outlook and values and political power dominated all aspects of local life. Though we lived in Idaho, just across the border from Utah, our cultural, commercial, and media connections, directed southward to Salt Lake City, had an unquestionable Mormon slant. After I served a thirty-month proselyting mission as a young man in Denmark during the mid-1950s, Sandra and I were married in the Logan LDS temple.

Under the influence of this religious and local cultural background, we reared four sons, participating regularly as a family in Latter-day Saint wards and stakes where we lived. Eventually three of our sons filled foreign proselyting missions for the church, an indication that Mormon theology and practice were strong forces in their lives.

There was, to be sure, something of a liberal interpretation of Mormon thought and culture in our home. My education in the humanities and work as a university professor made me doctrinally unorthodox in the eyes of some, and Sandra's evolution as an artist and her moderate feminist persuasions similarly widened her view of our Mormon heritage. But for both of us these developments were gradual and did not conflict, in our eyes at least, with those aspects of Mormon thought we regarded as valuable in our sons' upbringing.

This was the family ground in which Brad grew up.

As students of American religion know, Mormons are Christians with several important doctrinal differences from the Christian mainstream. Orthodox Mormons assert that Christ's original church disappeared after several centuries of apostasy, that the legitimate priesthood of God was withdrawn from the earth as a result, that through the prophet Joseph Smith the Church of Jesus Christ of Latter-day Saints was restored to the earth in 1830 along with indispensable priesthood keys. They consider this the "one true church," the only repository of the power to perform essential saving ordinances for all humankind. Moreover, Mormons believe that "as man is, God once was; and as God is, man may become."

I cite these beliefs, albeit superficially, simply to explain the strong insular tendencies of Mormonism and to suggest how powerfully it demands obedience to its doctrines and conformity with its lifestyle; how powerfully it demands commitment to building the kingdom of God; how powerfully it prescribes self-discipline and self-improvement within its parameters.

To grow up a Latter-day Saint is similar in some ways to growing up Catholic or Jew. Like these sister religions, Mormonism loads substantial guilt onto those who acknowledge its authority but do not, for whatever reason, conform to its ideology. Structured communal practices reinforce these pressures. To the extent that one allows it to do so, Mormonism absorbs one's time and attention, claiming to have answers for virtually all of life's great questions, and programs for addressing virtually all spiritual and social needs.

To be raised Mormon is to be subjected to a formidable process of indoctrination. Sunday school, Primary, Aaronic Priesthood activity, daily seminary instruction during high school years, a variety of special worship services and youth conferences: all this teaching machinery, insisting on the uniqueness of Mormon identity and its accompanying responsibilities, works on the minds and develops loyalties in young Latter-day Saints. They are taught to regard themselves proudly as "a peculiar people." It is not surprising then that many of them are characterized by moral earnestness.

Latter-day Saints stress the importance of strong families. There is no place in the highest heaven for singles, members are told. It is taken for granted that young people will eventually marry and found families of their own.

If a Mormon youth has keen moral sensibilities to start with, all of this intense environment and training can accumulate in a pretty heavy load of baggage.

Take a boy like Brad, naturally sensitive, respectful of his parents. Let him grow up in a loving home, which makes him want to reciprocate the love and loyalty he feels there. Let him have a full dose of church instruction from its varied sources, though such teaching occasionally rubs against the grain of his common sense. Give him a peer group of Mormon friends who, during the emotionally vulnerable teen years, are daily subjected to highly orthodox seminary instruction. Let him in that environment develop strong peer group loyalties. Then watch to see what develops for that powerfully conditioned youth when an element of inescapable, shocking nonconformity enters the equation.

Brad was twenty when he told us that he was gay. This announcement caught me by surprise and left me dubious, first of all because his strong-willed temperament and his broad-shouldered physique hardly fit the common stereotype. But there was a second and even more compelling reason for me to deny the validity of his assertion: I accepted the prevailing view of the church that homosexuality is a perverse "choice" of lifestyle, an impulse that can be overcome. With sufficient time to sort out his experience, surely a decent young man like Brad would not ultimately make such a choice. My son a queer? No. I had known him too long, too well to believe he really wanted such an identity. I felt certain that if he were patient he would come to recognize his assumption as fallacious and develop normal heterosexual desire, leading to marriage and a family.

Though I regarded myself at that time as broadminded and tolerant, homosexuality was a phenomenon about which I had powerful biases and little information. I told Brad that he could not have found a posture more difficult for me to accept. His mother was deeply troubled as well. We had not thought it possible that a home like ours could produce a gay son. Had she, she worried, been responsible in some way for his becoming homosexual? For a long time we denied, hoping for change, hoping that some girl, the right girl, would come along and bowl Brad over. Meanwhile, with heavy hearts and confused feelings, we started to study homosexuality, reading, observing, listening to any who we thought could help us sort it all out. It was arduous, slow work, especially since we undertook it in the closet.

But, of course, Brad's difficulties started long before his twentieth birthday. He had been aware from early years in grade school that his sexual attraction was toward males, and if early on that knowledge was less than fully realized, with his advance into adolescence and a series of unspoken crushes on male athlete friends, he could not ultimately deny the reality of an inclination that was, in the context of his world, unthinkable.

In those late teen years Brad read everything about homosexuality he could get his hands on. He knew, of course, the church's position, that homosexuality is unnatural and inappropriate (since it does not lead to marriage and family), that homosexual acts are grave sins, that homosexual marriage is a contradiction in terms. He had therefore two culturally acceptable alternatives: live celibately or renounce his mistaken choice and find a way to enter into a faithful heterosexual marriage.

Through his reading Brad became aware of contrary views, namely that homosexual orientation is not chosen, that it likely has a biological basis. This seemed consistent with what he knew of his own feelings. His intellect and his self-respect wanted to accept these assertions. But faced with the church's moral authority, he was filled with doubt.

Like many young homosexuals, his ego was battered.* His high

---

*The difficulty and the damage experienced by gays in a conservative culture are suggested in the following: "From their youth the seeds of low self-esteem are planted. From both adults and peers they hear the deprecating epithets, the scornful aspersions, the biased misinformation about gays which

school journals reveal poignantly the continuing turmoil he felt as he tried to suppress his feelings and to imitate the social attitudes and dating patterns of his friends. They reveal that he prayed long and fervently that God would help him change, that he promised to do anything necessary to bring about such change. Only later did we come to understand how difficult his teen years had been, how filled with confusion, conflict, and self-hatred. We did know that frequently he had struggled with nagging bouts of depression which worried us but for which we had no explanation except teenage doldrums. We did not know how deeply alienated he felt from his religion, to which he wanted to be faithful; from his friends, who did not really know him; even from his family, whose expectations for him were not compatible, he was sure, with what he knew he was.

These inner conflicts reached a crisis point when at age nineteen he had to decide whether to serve a two-year proselyting mission. The official position of the Mormon hierarchy is that all young males should accept a mission call. Health permitting, there are ostensibly no really valid excuses for not doing so, and powerful pressures—institutional, familial, peer—to help bring this about. It is not easy to say no, but finally that was Brad's answer. Though he had not, at nineteen, engaged in homosexual relations and thus was presum-

---

cause them to feel contemptible. They struggle to understand their difference in an environment which demands conformity. They hide their feelings from the world, even from loved ones, and hate themselves for this deception. . . . They read books confirming their fear that they are flawed or mentally ill. And when they desperately need to turn to the church for comfort and assurance, it proclaims its 'love for the sinner,' its 'condemnation of the sin.' Ironically, the more orthodox the individual, the more he believes he is wicked, and the more he suffers from this institutional repudiation of his identity. His 'tainted' sexuality seems to him the central fact of his existence and colors all facets of his life" (H. Wayne Schow, "Homosexuality, Mormon Doctrine, and Christianity," *Sunstone*, Feb. 1990, 12).

ably worthy in this and other respects, how could he without violating himself represent the church that denied the legitimacy of his deeply-felt identity.

Brad's first two college years were dominated by tortured internal dialogue. It became explicit in the pages of his journals wherein one can read the blow-by-counterblow of these arguments, his attempts to believe in the theoretical possibility of positive rewards in gay relationships, his simultaneous recognition of the seemingly insupportable cost of such nonconformity. In college, especially after leaving Pocatello, he turned increasingly by inclination and necessity to new friends who helped him see beyond the implicit views of his narrowly-orthodox high school peer group. In those two years he moved a long way, doubtless thrust forward by the cumulative unreleased pressures of his teen years.

When at the end of his sophomore year Brad came out to us, he knew it was a risk. Doubtless he hoped we'd be accepting, or, failing that, perhaps he had faith we would eventually come around. In any case, he had made a courageous decision. He knew there was a truth about himself that he must accept, and that that truth must in some undeniable way shape his life. He needed our support.

I wish we had been able to give it to him immediately, unqualifiedly. We couldn't. Oh, there was no outward anger, there were no threats of disowning. He knew, I am sure, that we loved him. But we could not say, "Listen to the voice within you, Brad, and follow it. Go with our blessing: find and nourish who you really are." We couldn't say it, for we did not trust his inner voice. We were products of the lessons we had learned through life that could not be unlearned overnight. How could we give him license to become something we had been taught to abominate.*

---

*In the years that followed, my view of homosexuality and its theological implications changed significantly. Based on wide reading together with direct observation of the numerous homosexuals I have come to know, I now believe

A few months later Brad left to find a different kind of life in Los Angeles. With conflicted emotions, we drove to Salt Lake City to help him move out of his apartment and ship his belongings. We said our goodbyes in an ambience of dazed unbelief.

The decisions he made that spring and summer marked him with tragic potential. Perhaps that sounds hyperbolic. Many young people have broken with their inherited culture with results not necessarily tragic. What I want to say is that the preconditions for tragedy were coalescing. Here was an especially intense young man, earnest and passionate and idealistic, wanting so badly to find moral and philosophical justification for his life in the face of society's disapproval. The situation called for an easygoing pragmatist, which Brad could never be.

He knew that in coming out and going to live in the gay culture of West Hollywood he was burning bridges. His mother's and my response at the time was qualified at best, the attitudes of his younger brothers highly uncertain, and he was almost certainly cutting himself off from all but a few of his closely knit extended family. Moreover, he was effectually breaking with his church, a major decision, for fellowship in the church is regarded by Mormons as indispensable for salvation. Not least of all, he was sepa-

---

that this orientation has a biological basis, that one does not choose or learn to be homosexual. Such a premise changes the ethics of homosexual behavior, and changes similarly the ethics of response by the heterosexual majority toward this significant *natural* minority. I believe that our sexuality, however oriented, is one of God's important gifts, with the potential to enrich our lives. From a Christian perspective, we should judge its expression by the fruits it bears. Just as we assess heterosexual relationships in terms of commitment and whether such relationships contribute to long-term growth and holistic well-being, so we should assess homosexual relationships. The question is thus not *whether* one is homosexual but *how*. Biblical passages that bear on the question of homosexuality are not free of contextual cultural bias. In the light of Christian teaching, we should love all persons as God has created them and assist them in realizing their unique potential.

rating himself from the culture and lifestyle he had known growing up in Idaho.

Did he feel ambivalent about these decisions? Of course. But having decided he could not live authentically in his old world, he felt considerable exhilaration, as when in a risky situation one says with some bravado, "What the hell, let's go for it!" He did not at twenty understand that deeply ingrained loyalties would not allow him easily to lay aside emotional bonds of an upbringing such as his. In this he was unwise, as are other tragic individuals who think as they embark on a path leading to extremity that the strength of their desire will overcome obstacles to its fulfillment.

Los Angeles beckoned with all its dazzling hedonism. After a relationship with first one, then another lover proved unstable, he drifted increasingly into the bar scene. Drugs, which had never previously been part of his life, contributed to the dionysian atmosphere in which he was caught up. "Dad, I'm in a new world. You can't believe how my consciousness is raised." After a time he was teetering on the brink of addiction, and his friends were worried about him. Then came a bout with hepatitis. We did not know until later how far things had gone with him.

Meanwhile, he had sense enough to see he had gotten into a bad state. He exerted his will, got drug use under control, watched his health, and moderated his behavior generally. Since he was not making a lot of money and was at the same time taking night classes at UCLA, he needed considerable discipline to get through his illness and at the same time make ends meet. He didn't fully reveal these difficulties to us. It was characteristic of him that, having gotten himself into a mess, he intended to extricate himself by his own means.

Best of all from our point of view, he began to realize that underlying gay life in West Hollywood was a deep-seated nihilism, that the frenzied activity of the gay bars was an attempt to cover despair. He saw increasingly in many around him—and in himself—the effects of alienation, pessimism, and hopelessness about the future. On several occasions he considered suicide (a couple of

phone calls to us in the small hours of the morning were frightening). For all of its excitement, he understood gradually that the
aesthetic, hedonistic culture dominant in Los Angeles was incompatible with his real needs. Somehow, though it meant leaving a
supportive community, he had to reincorporate himself into the
mainstream. "Much as I love this place, I've got to get out of here,
to somewhere less distracting; I've got to get back into school."

About this time, after three and a half years in L.A., he became
acquainted with a young man who also had grown up in Idaho.
Drew had been living in Honolulu for a year or so, and, like Brad,
he left Idaho originally because, as a homosexual, he was not
accepted there. Brad was not prepared to return to the mountain
west, but by joining with Drew he could leave L.A. and move to an
attractive, smaller urban environment in Hawaii. With Drew he
thought he could find a way back to the simpler, more wholesome
values he associated with his Idaho upbringing. His enthusiasm for
this fresh direction was so typical, another zenith in his psychological pattern of roller coaster highs and lows. But we did not attempt
to dissuade him. Anything that takes him away from L.A., we
thought, will be an improvement.

Alas, the interlude with Drew did not prove to be paradise. On
the positive side, the two young men enjoyed excursions about the
island in their free time, hikes in the hills, swimming in the ocean.
For Brad, who had been searching for a new kind of religious faith,
the exposure to natural Hawaii was at times a mystical experience,
an encounter with deities of wind and sky and sea. His spiritual
imagination was fed by this exotic environment. Unfortunately, he
began to realize that Drew was not his soul mate. Brad felt uncomfortable with the religious simplicities to which Drew was drawn,
and Drew did not share Brad's intense love of the arts. Their
romance sprang up quickly, intensely, but planted in shallow soil,
it soon wilted in the tropical sun. Sadly, this painful recognition of
an inadequate fit came at a juncture when Brad badly needed a
secure and loving relationship.

Initially, Brad found employment in Honolulu as a landscape

gardener. After several months he applied for a position with a firm that specialized in sophisticated advertising graphics. Underqualified for the computerized work, he talked his way into the job on a probationary basis, brashly confident that he could pick it up quickly. Suddenly he was under tension in a pressured environment. At the end of a month, the owner told him the experiment was not working and let him go. This defeat caught him at a low point. First another failed relationship and now fired! The dismissal magnified in retrospect every setback he had ever experienced, every thwarted ambition. The Hawaiian idyll had turned ugly. He was devastated. Concerned about his health, both physical and mental, we persuaded him to come home for awhile.

It took several months for him to pull himself back together. He had lived so intensely during those four years away, had poured himself so passionately into his quest for a way that he could live, had taken risks, cast prudence aside to see if he could seize love, some purpose, and self-acceptance—and at this juncture it all came crashing down. His badly bruised spirit is revealed in the pathos of a journal entry just before leaving Hawaii: "Please don't let everything I've loved so far be a mistake, as it seems in their eyes."

I am laboring (albeit superficially) over these biographical details not for their own sake so much as to show how Brad pursued vigorously, if not always wisely, self-realization against the grain of his culture, how he insisted on his right to be himself according to conditions thrust on him by his biology and his particular place and moment in history, and how those circumstances continually assaulted and undermined his confidence. I am attempting to convey my perception that if well into his twenties Brad was still trying to find himself, it was because, given his character, his situation, and the choices that flowed from their combination, there was for him no easy road to contentment. Perhaps I have not emphasized sufficiently his romantic temperament. What I hope to suggest is that in his case the nemesis of AIDS came along as a by-product of his insistent quest.

In September Brad enrolled in Landscape Architecture at Utah

State University. He toiled at the curriculum for two years, exhilarated by the aesthetic, botanical, and social facets of the discipline. He struggled some with the mathematical requirements where his confidence had always been shaky. He lived in a dormitory and was a floor resident assistant.

His life in Logan was characterized by continuous intense ambivalence. While he loved the physical environment—a striking campus positioned against steeply rising mountains and overlooking the pastoral valley where he had been born—it seemed to him that religious provincialism dominated both his campus contacts and the community generally. He hated that. Doubtless he was hypersensitive to Mormon orthodoxy and not altogether fair in his sweeping condemnations of it. He railed against what seemed the smug and unquestioning attitudes of his student peers. Reluctantly, he forced himself back into the closet, feeling he could not afford to run the social, academic, and physical risks that openness would entail. He felt his authenticity sharply compromised. Thus, Logan was, from a psychological point of view, altogether the wrong place for him to be. There his tendency toward depression would be greatly exacerbated. But he reasoned that this alienated life was temporary and could be gotten through.

It would prove more difficult than he imagined. His journals describe debilitating moodswings resulting at least in part from the contradictions of his personal situation. "I feel as if I am living my life in a vacuum—no friends, no real stimulating conversation, no night life, no confidante, nowhere to get away." Frustrated with his isolation and increasingly depressed at the prospect of a continued sentence of residence in Logan, he began to develop ominous health problems late in his second year. As the semester wore on, he felt less strong, and he muddled through something like an appendicitis attack without bothering to seek any medical help.

When he returned home in June, we were surprised that he had lost weight. Within a couple of weeks he was hospitalized for an appendectomy, then a return to overcome a postoperative infection. Tests showed irregularities in his blood, including sharply reduced

T-cell levels. The specter of AIDS loomed, but we clung to the possibility of other causes. It was too ironic to think that after his having abandoned gay life in Los Angeles, after his almost monkish retreat to northern Utah, he might now have AIDS. As the summer progressed, the multiple symptoms of ARC (AIDS-related complex) presented themselves—loss of appetite, more pronounced weight loss, low grade fever, night sweats, fatigue, sleeplessness, coughing.

By late October Brad developed increasingly alarming respiratory difficulties. Was this pneumocystis pneumonia, a confirmation of AIDS? Fatalistically, he resisted hospitalization, but when it became clear in early November that he must either be admitted to the hospital or die (and he was too ill to know this) we simply could not accept the latter alternative and called the ambulance. Twenty hours later his blood oxygen level fell to a point incompatible with life. Earlier he had said emphatically that he did not want to be kept alive by mechanical means. Again, faced with his death as the alternative, we agonized, then gave our permission to employ a respirator. Later we learned that without Brad's cooperation the breathing tube could not have been efficiently inserted in the perilously short time left. For ten days we kept a family vigil at his bedside. Neither his doctors nor we really expected him to survive that ordeal in the Intensive Care Unit.

He did. Thanksgiving and Christmas were joyous holidays for us that year. Brad began to recover his appetite, began to gain back some weight. The AIDS, now officially confirmed, was in remission. We knew, of course, about the formal death sentence in that diagnosis, but hope revives with the most slender encouragement. If he could keep alive for a year or two, perhaps the research breakthrough would come, a cure be found. In January, with renewed will to live, he felt well enough to enroll in a journalism course at Idaho State University.

"April," Eliot wrote, "is the cruelest month." That was when the tide turned, when the insidious disease reasserted its power. It was a crucial turn, stamped with inexorability. Brad knew, and we knew, that at this late stage he could not afford to give up much ground.

AIDS is a relentless aggressor. It takes a person apart incrementally. From the toes to the brain, no part of the body—muscles, nerves, organs—is safe from its ravages. One fights it on one front, only to have it attack elsewhere. Gradually, the incursions assume cumulative proportions. In May and June Brad struggled against a growing barrage of ailments, the most obvious of which were nausea, weakness, and extreme fatigue. Above all, he struggled to keep believing that he could hang on, that if he did he might still find some measure of quality in his life.

In late June he managed to finish a month-long history course at ISU but did it like a battered boxer in the late rounds, mostly on instinct and guts. The physical slide continued. His normally well-defined muscles lost tone. He grew more pale, gaunt, listless. Walking became increasingly difficult and painful, his vision was affected, and there were two ominous brain lesions. He stopped driving the Dodge Challenger he had been so proud of, knowing that his reflexes were no longer sufficiently reliable. One day in a grocery store he tried to fill out a check and, humiliated, could not remember how to do it.

I was with him one day in early August when he asked his doctor for an honest estimate of his chances, and that kind man, who had become Brad's friend and buoyed up his spirits on many occasions in the course of their cooperative effort, replied: "If the rapid decline we are now seeing continues, it is unlikely you can go on for very long."

That was a difficult recognition. A day or so later, Brad told us he had decided to dispose of his possessions. He wanted to make sure that the things he had lovingly chosen over the years would get into the hands of individuals who would value them too—his combined edition of Tolkien, his Beardsley, his Bible, his fairy tale collections, and numerous other books; his classical records and funky collection of popular music; his prints, photographs, posters, and small art pieces; a few antiques. He wanted to do it while his mind was still clear.

In early September his best friend Scott came from southern California to visit. We drove up into the mountains together to see the scenes Brad had loved, to walk along the clear mountain creeks where flaming scrub maples and bold-yellow aspens defined the water course, where the views over the narrow valley to mountains beyond were sharply etched in the clear air of autumn. He could not walk far. A few days afterward, his youngest brother Ted left to be a missionary in Uruguay. These were significant farewells.

I cannot say that he spent those last months in a sustained heroic effort to stay alive. Rather, he was caught in a terrible ambivalence, vacillating between the will to live and the will to die. In either direction, the operative word is will. I had supposed that when a person gives up the fight for life, what follows is a passive drift toward death. I should have known that Brad could never drift passively. When the experimental drug AZT was publicized in early fall as a means of arresting AIDS, he quickly made arrangements to secure it in a last effort to seize back momentum. But by the time the red tape was all cut, a month had passed, and his case was too far advanced for the drug to be efficacious. So, if death it was to be, he would have it on his own terms, with some measure of dignity. Suicide was a possibility he considered seriously for the time when his condition became incontrovertibly hopeless. Ultimately he decided to face it out, to let nature run its course. But as he approached the end, he determined, with the concurrence of his physician, that he would cease taking the antibiotic that helped him in his rearguard struggle against opportunistic infections, and that if the end came at home or in hospital, no aggressive measures would be taken to keep him alive, only provision of what comfort was possible.

He was no saint, no perfect stoic during those last months. He ran the gamut of emotions. From his volatile nature spilled dejection, irony, irritability, nostalgia, islands of humor, and—not least—sharp anger against the utter absurdity of it all, anger that sometimes lashed those around him. Dylan Thomas's line, "Rage, rage against the dying of the light," exactly characterizes those moods. The light died literally in one of his eyes a few weeks before the end, extinguished by one of those brain lesions. But the mind that could momentarily forget how to make out a check was still capable of insightful reflection as counterpoint against the rage.

And we others stood by like a Sophoclean chorus, filled with lamentation, knowing that our pitiful words were inadequate response to the passion in which the central figure of this drama toiled. This was a trial of spirit that somehow gathered up the personal suffering of a lifetime. And now his struggle had come down to, was epitomized in, this life-and-death wrestling with AIDS.

During the last month and a half the wasted legs would not support him. A wheel chair was necessary for his movement about the house or outside for medical treatment. Before our eyes, he became physically much like an aged man, with thinned hair, sharpened visage. Because of the pain of movement, he found baths difficult and exhausting. We worked out a way that he could shower. From a piece of lumber, we fashioned a seat that could be laid across the edges of the tub. I would help him remove his pajamas, lift him from the wheelchair to the edge of the seat, then assist him to ease the aching legs very slowly, very carefully over the edge. And then he could manage. For me it became a deeply moving ritual. Two men, son and father, were bonded together in a matrix of pain, humility, frustration, and love. The warm water that soothed and cleansed him seemed sacramental.

Ironically, Brad's quest for religious truth was a core element in his tragic impasse. This might surprise anyone exposed simply to Brad's pointed, occasionally caustic, irony. But his search for self demanded idealistic validation. When years earlier it had become clear that the religion of his upbringing would not accommodate his identity, he was reluctantly set adrift. The search for an alternative religion led him to consider ascetic Christianity, pantheism, oriental mysticism, new age philosophy. Even his drug experience in Los Angeles was fraught with overtones of a religious quest. But none of these, nor eclectic combinations of them, finally answered his need.

I think it a credit to him that as the sands of his life ran out he disdained to compromise his intellectual honesty or his experiential truth. However much solace traditional faith might have provided, he went as an agnostic to face whatever lies beyond. At the very bottom of his religious consciousness there remained, I think, a soft sympathy with important facets of Mormon theology. I have wondered more than a few times since his death whether the religious upbringing we gave him was, on balance, more help or hindrance to him in his life. Whatever the answer to this question, that upbringing was a large part of the cross he bore.

And so as time passes, I perceive more clearly in Brad's life the ambience of tragedy. He is not a large scale tragic protagonist, to be sure. But in the face of forces inimical to his just desires, he did not flinch or turn aside. He had wanted so much—love, authenticity, beauty, achievement, self-knowledge, self-acceptance—and after his fashion he had pursued them uncompromisingly. Beginning with his boyhood conflicts, continuing through the trials of his young manhood, and concluding with the body- and mind-sapping illness, his ordeal had extended sufficiently long for his passion and courage to shine forth. In the end he had run out of time, or perhaps there would never have been enough time, to reconcile the inescapable contradictions in his life. But that he never gave up trying demonstrates the largeness of his spirit. In the furnace of this effort was forged the hard-won moral insight from which he looked back and judged what he had done.

Could the outcome have been avoided? Perhaps if those around him had been more enlightened, more accepting, he might have found a companion nearer home, might not have chosen self-exile to escape intolerance, might thereby have avoided the path of alienation and self-destruction. Had he followed the advice he was given, for example, and accepted docilely the hand dealt him, been patient, and remained celibate, he would still be alive. But if he had demanded less from life, he would not have been Brad, and the question of tragedy would be irrelevant.

That was just it: he made demands. That was the essence of his attitude. If that was his flaw, it does him credit. If in the last analysis I persist in seeing him as tragic, in seeing his ordinary life as more than ordinary, it is for the reason that he could not—or would not—accept the either/or premises that life thrust on him, would not give up on the one hand his natural necessity (and right) to be gay, including the extremes of his exploration of that identity, or on the other hand his need for respect from the idealistic culture that was formative in his development. He could not have it both ways. His losing bout with AIDS seems to symbolize that fact. But I doubt, had he the chance to live his life again, that he would do it differently.

Speaking as a member of the chorus, I stand in the aftermath troubled by the inscrutability of much that I have witnessed. In this case, the conditions of mortality did not seem perfectly fair, nor easily borne. And I am dismayed that the cultural values we humans have created so often unnecessarily place stumbling blocks for our companions rather than easing their burdens. But as a father I now contemplate my son's responses with respect. Though he experienced deep discouragement along his way, there was nevertheless a resilient toughness in the core of him, and I do not think he was ever beaten in spirit, not even in the last difficult days.

II. Entries from Brad's Journals, 1975-86

At the age of fifteen, Brad began to keep a personal journal. Together with friends from school, he was encouraged by his high school LDS seminary teacher to do so. For an introspective youth, it was an activity congenial to his personality and soon became an established part of his routine. During the remainder of his life he filled seven notebooks and bound journals. They constitute a vivid revelation of his character and temperament, a record of his evolving values and of his quest for self-understanding and personal acceptance. It is ironic that the life path his journals reveal moved dramatically away from the course charted in his seminary instruction.

As with many personal journals, there are lapses in Brad's entries. That those silences seem so regrettable is a measure of the engaging quality of what he did write. The value derives in part from the candor. During his high school years, Brad wrestled as most diarists do with finding an acceptable persona. The desire to be approved in terms of family or religious or social values censors, consciously or unconsciously, what he records. It is not so much that he expects his entries to be read, at least not immediately; rather he is so conscious of external expectations that he reflects the persona he feels compelled to assume in his life.

21

Year by year, little by little, he moves toward more honest statements (at times startlingly candid) and more insightful assessment of his feelings. He makes no effort to hide or disguise his faults, misbehaviors, desires. The writing is truly done for himself, a way of seeking to clarify what is confusing in his life. It is as if the stakes grow larger and he must drop any posturing. This together with his growing intellectual sophistication results in a record as complex as its subject.

Filled with contradictions, paradoxes, polar tensions, it reveals a young man with a mercurial temperament whose perplexing moodswings are unpredictable to himself as well as to others, and for whom as a result life's joys and sorrows are extreme. It shows a gentle romantic whose sensitivities are encouraged by the sentimental side of his religious upbringing. At the same time, it reveals a rebel, an obedient son who nevertheless bristles against authority, whose dark side causes him to be irritated with those who are complacently comfortable, including family and friends. And because the environment in which he matures implicitly urges suppression of that dark side, his journal becomes a place where he can express it, an escape valve from sweetness and reason. His journal is, as he once wrote, "a place to trash things."

These journals are remarkable for the degree to which they exclude the external world, or, more precisely, they reflect it only indirectly as externalities contribute to his feelings. If he refers to clean sheets or symphonies or friends or the weather, such references are couched in terms of his enjoyment or displeasure. The focus is primarily and consistently inward. He can be extraordinarily self-reflective, subjectively analytical. Repeatedly he dreams of becoming a significant artist, but he is so preoccupied with personal dilemmas that he cannot marshall the energy and discipline needed for artistic endeavor. His ability to act effortlessly and spontaneously is repeatedly undermined by his cerebral recognition of complexity, ambiguity, irony. Early on in the journals one sees frequent contradictory assessments.

Youthfully naive, he is probably not aware of a number of them. Yet they derive often from his unconscious ambivalence. As he grows older, he becomes more aware, but the ambiguities continue.

His self-criticism is severe and sometimes verges on morbidity. He tries almost desperately to love himself but finds it difficult to do. Why? The idealism of his upbringing, which so many of us take with a grain of salt, he takes seriously. He is intelligent enough to see the contradictions between the moral ideal and the real, but he requires that they be reconciled. His problem is a conscience too highly developed, too dominating, and when he tries to throw it out and live with abandon, he can only temporarily escape the guilt. All of which seems clearly apparent in the record he left. It is painful for me as his father to recognize these effects of moral training that was well intended. I find myself wishing somehow that we had instead trained him as a picaro. He could then doubtless have borne his life more lightly.

In nothing is the perplexity of his life so evident as in the matter of his sexuality. This subject dominates the journals. He does not begin to discuss overtly his homosexual orientation until he is nearly nineteen and entering college, but it is clear both from veiled comments in earlier entries and from what he subsequently has to say that he agonizes over this taboo not only throughout his teenage years but to the end of his life. The issue throws him off stride in virtually all aspects of his personal adjustment.

Repeatedly he tries to persuade himself that he can fall in love with a woman. Marriage and children are so important to his programming for a happy life that anything else is virtually unthinkable. As he acknowledges his desire for gay relationships, he continues to try to work out scenarios in which such a lifestyle can be reconciled morally with fatherhood. He recognizes the virtual impossibility of this but clings to its remote possibility.

How sad it seems to see him struggling to accept his gay orientation but always stymied at a deeper level because of guilt and awareness of establishment disapproval. He wrestles the matter back and forth, belaboring the same points, believing his own arguments but then in moments of self-doubt denying them. Cursed—or blessed—with a powerful libido, he could not find a satisfactory and lasting outlet for it, and sex became indeed the unceasing thorn in his flesh.

Readers will doubtless interpret his dilemma and its causes in various ways, but two things are clear. For whatever reasons there is a pronounced and genuine homosexual element in his sexuality, and he suffers profoundly as a result of his inability to overcome conflicts occasioned by his church's and society's powerful disapproval.

The journal entries selected here constitute only a small part of the seven books. Regrettably, I have omitted much detail relating to friends, schooling, family relations, work, leisure activities, aesthetic interests, and the hedonistic life in Los Angeles. Even in representing the major themes of the journals I have had to be selective. As a result, one loses part of the documentary power of these manuscripts. One loses also some of the pathos of frequent iteration. Nevertheless, readers should be aware that each entry is in some way broadly representative and can therefore be multiplied. Regrettably, the gaps in his account remain, those hiatuses when the writing stopped.

Traced in the pages of his journals, Brad's life developed along a path that was, if not inevitable, then at least, given his temperament and cultural positioning, somewhat predictable. I have often asked myself what, if he had lived longer, the remainder of his life would have been. Perhaps it might have paralleled in some ways the development of his prose in the journals. It is pleasing to observe his growth as a writer over those years. The enthusiastic scribbler of the early notebooks was gradually replaced by both a more mature stylist and a shrewder, more insightful observer of himself and others. He did this substantially on his own, without the benefit of formal writing instruction and criticism beyond college composition. The development was a result of his reading, his life experience, and his passion for expression. I like to think that his life, like his writing, would have moved beyond its turbulent apprenticeship, that he would have gradually found self-assurance and a comfortable standing place. Perhaps his evolution can benefit others who travel somewhere along a similar path of development.

———

[Age 16—sophomore year, high school]

JUNE 21, 1975:Tom and I went over to Kimberly's tonight. It was pretty fun. We sat around talking and laughing for quite a long time. I think that I could really like her. An awful lot. I don't know. I am really relaxed around her, and I can be myself. Sometimes I think that maybe she might like me. I don't know though. I probably just imagine it, but there are times I sure hope I don't!! The thing about it is that I don't really want to go with anyone. I just want to find that one special girl and just become terrific good friends—but still be more than that.

JULY 19, 1975: How empty my life seems at this time, for the spirit of the Lord has left me. It is gone for reasons that I know of but of which I shall not write. It makes me feel so awful. When I try to pray there is nothing but blank!! Nothing.

JULY 27, 1975 [Excerpt from letter to a friend]: I'm really getting excited about going on a [two-year full-time proselyting] mission [for the LDS church]. I can't wait until I'm old enough to get my call. I don't care where I go, but I wouldn't mind leaving the country and going to Israel or Russia or China. Those would be my preferences, in that order.

I want to teach the gospel to people who don't have it. I want to do that so much. It's not so much that I want to convert them to Mormonism, but rather I would like to teach them the gospel of Jesus Christ. I know that sounds strange, but it makes sense to me at least. I want to do that work for the Lord. I know he would help me. I also know that it would be very hard, but that it would help me grow.

AUGUST 3, 1975: Tom and I have decided to organize a street dance. We've been recording good songs on tapes with his new reel-to-reel, and we'll have to see if everybody would like to help. It would be great. Tom is such a special person to me. We do everything together. But I'm so afraid that what happened to the friendship with George will happen again. And I don't want this friendship ever to stop. I hate to start getting close to people because if you stop being friends, you can really get hurt. I really do love him an awful lot.

Friends and friendships are deluxe things when it comes down to it. Especially when you are real close. You learn to love your closest friends just like family. And that's how I want it to stay. I don't think I could give up my friendships with Tom and Wendy and Kimberly for all the world. They mean too much to me.

AUGUST 12, 1975: There are so many times lately that I become confused and disoriented. Times that I suddenly can't think straight, as though someone has taken me and shaken me upside down for an hour and all my thoughts have slipped into a jumbled mess. It isn't a sickness or anything of that sort, but there are times when it seems as if everything rushes to my head all at once and demands to be thought about right then. But that doesn't exactly present the clearest picture possible. . . .

I want to take some art classes next year at school, and I would really like to be able to draw better. I wish I could find a teacher who would get in and work with me and help me develop at it. I think I have the potential to be a fairly good artist. This is also the way I feel about the piano. I would like to start taking lessons again, from someone who could really work with me. Also, I wish I could take some writing classes at school. I wish I could do that a little better too.

——

[Junior year, high school]

SEPTEMBER 10, 1975: Tonight Bishop Staheli called me and said he would like to talk to me for a while. So I went to see him and he asked me to be president of the mutual program in our ward [Mutual Improvement Association for youth]. I couldn't believe it. I haven't been to mutual for about six months. But he said that the choice hadn't been made quickly, that much thought had gone into it. I accepted.

I'm so excited. I can't wait. I'm going to give it everything I'm worth. I will be in charge of everything. It is really going to be a challenge. I'm so thankful for this calling. Now I have a reason to go to mutual. Before it was so boring to me that I just quit going. I surely hope and pray the Lord will bless me and help me do this job well.

OCTOBER 13, 1975: I have just finished the *Book of Mormon*. It was wonderful. . . . I put the promise to the test, and it worked (you know, Moroni 10:4). I prayed twice, and I still wanted to pray more. I was so happy. . . . I prayed for forgiveness also of the many terrible sins that I've committed. And this time I *know* he forgave me. I asked that his spirit would come to me and that from this time on it would never leave me, ever! It's left before and there would only be a great empty gap inside of me. I asked that I would be able to resist the temptations put before me by Satan and that I would never do anything again that would give the spirit cause to leave.

OCTOBER 22, 1975: Today I am filled with a joy for life. A real, true, overflowing love of life. I don't know when I've felt more contented. I'll try to explain why. Today was Dad's birthday. Well, it started to snow just slightly early this morning. Then later on in the afternoon it began to come hurrying down as if those snowflakes were late for an appointment. Really snowing hard in other words! The radio said that it was going to freeze, so Mom decided we'd better dig up all the carrots and beets out of the garden. So when Dad got home, guess what we did? We all went out in the mud and the cold and the blizzard, and the whole family dug up carrots and beets for quite a while. It was so cold. But we were doing it as a family. (Now here is a place I can't describe.) It struck me as being neat.

Then because Mom didn't have time to cook a big dinner, we just had some frozen pies. I remember when we came in from the garden all cold and wet how warm the house was and how good those pies smelled baking. It was great. So we didn't have a fancy dinner to celebrate Dad's birthday like we usually do. And then me and Roger and Mike had to hurry and go to road show [drama] practice and mutual, so we gave Dad his two small presents which weren't very much and sang happy birthday to him and hurried on our way. I know that this birthday was special to Dad. It wasn't big, but it was *special*.

At mutual Roger and Suzanne Staheli (the bishop's daughter and Roger's girlfriend) and I just ran around in the snow outside the church and rolled and laughed and played. We ate the snow and threw it at each other and all of us got wet. It was dark but light the way it always is when it snows. We knocked all the snow off the trees so they wouldn't break and made tracks and ran around. It was so much fun and we were so happy. (Here is another place that I can't describe!) It was just the time and the place and the snow and the cold and the dark night but light sky.

And then when we came home, I was struck again by the moment. The house was so warm and inviting. Mom and Dad sat in the living room watching the news, and outside the floodlights were on and I could see all the trees just loaded down with snow and so white and pretty. You've probably heard about winter fairylands, well this was one. I could see the snow coming down so heavy.

Everything was so wonderful and good. My parents, the lights on in the living room, the soft murmur of the TV, the snow outside, the heavy laden trees and the inviting warmth of the house. This all took place in just a second, but to me it was wonderful. We were all so content and happy. And then when everybody was going to bed, I turned off all the lights in the house and sat in the living room on the couch with the radio playing soft music and watched the snow fall. It was falling more gently now; it was so beautiful. And again I felt the security and peace.

And now I sit here alone in my room writing this messy scribble. I can feel God's spirit with me and about this house and know that he is watching over us. I hope that my children will someday be able to experience this happiness in much the same way. And I hope that their home and family will be as special to them as mine are to me.

APRIL 14, 1976: At times I feel so unhappy and dissatisfied with what I am, what I stand for and believe in, the things that I do, etc. I feel that my character is lacking, but when I try to pinpoint the places where this is so I find that I don't know how to change it. It seems to get up and run away from me. Sometimes I would like so very much to be able to lie down and go to sleep, and then wake up later and be able to start again. . . . There are things that I have done and things that I do now that seem to hang around my neck like a heavy stone, determined to pull me down till I drown.

I think a lot about forgiveness and about repentance. I wonder if there isn't something different to it than what the church says. It doesn't seem to agree with me the way they put it. I think that perhaps one has to forgive oneself instead of God doing the forgiving, for I think that we can be greater critics of ourselves than he will ever be. Heavenly Father loves us, but I think that many times we don't. Isn't that true? Sometimes I can't seem to forgive myself for things done a long time ago. It's not an easy thing, I guess it wasn't meant to be. But it can be so hard on one. . . . I remember the great struggles that I would have with [Satan], how it always brought me down very low to the point where I could not withstand his temptations and I gave in to him. I then classified myself as far lower than a Hindu "untouchable." I think that this has not been exactly healthy for my state of mind. But about Satan, I don't think he is always there prompting me. I wonder if he doesn't let us fight our own *natural* desires. I think that we attribute more to him than he deserves, make him a whipping boy. Perhaps he uses depression and fear as tools to accomplish what he wants. I do think that we can be "masters of our own fate." I believe that Heavenly Father has gotten to a point where he has mastered the most difficult problem he ever faced—himself. He, like us, chose to come to earth and had the same kinds of problems to overcome. He had sexual desires that he had to learn to control, he had a temper that had to be mastered, and so forth.

AUGUST 27, 1976: I find there is growing tension in myself about the church. I almost hate it. It's too confining, yet I am of it. It's too deeply set in me to be able to chuck it, though sometimes that's what I'd like to do. But the funny thing is, sometimes I almost work to make myself not find any of it agreeable. I find myself trying to be negative about it. Silly! I suppose that would be Satan's work. That's another thing I'm tired of. Him! He's always around. Why can't I be a gentle, believing, conforming church-lover like so many of the others. Sometimes it sounds so inviting. But it goes against my whole grain. It turns my guts over.

I am disgusted with myself too, over my inability to cope with temptation, my weak will power, my selfishness, my obstinacy, etc. That's not a very bright personal picture. I have so much self-confidence, ha ha! I wonder why I've turned out as I have. A mix-up.

———

[Senior year, high school]

AUGUST 30, 1976: Why am I so irritable? I can hardly stand to be around my family, they just get on my nerves something terrible. I want to get away from here, away from them. I know I'm acting immature. But I'm also getting tired of always worrying about that. I need to just straighten up! I need someone to shake me *good and hard*! I need to act my age. Snap to, Brad!

School started today. It's going to be a great last year, I think. My classes are good. They're all going to be interesting and fun. It sure is nice to be back home again and going to dear old Poky [Pocatello High School].

OCTOBER 25, 1976: My journal—sometimes I use it as my dumping ground, placing in it all the hateful, mean feelings inside me. I throw them away here. But other times it becomes my trusted friend. My one and only true listener. To it I bring my feelings of elation, of joy, emotions so full I am not able to carry them alone anymore.

APRIL 7, 1977 [after an extended description of the sights and sounds and smells of a spring evening]: I hear the breeze rustle far away, and then it comes nearer and nearer through the grass like a sleek animal, until I feel it pass across my face and tousle my hair. I can hear the cats playing in the grass above me. The bells around their necks tinkle as they cavort, as they carry out their mock attacks on each other. The evening star has just come out. I'll have to make a wish. I wish that my children will be able sometime in their lives to enjoy and love an evening as pleasant as this one is for me.

———

[After high school graduation]

JULY 30, 1977: I am fascinated by my growing up experience. I can see myself mellowing; I can roll with the punches so much easier now than say two years ago. I have found that I can cope with the constant onset of arrows and bombs in forms of school pressure, family, church, and love—and of course the ever-present, never-ceasing sexual drive. Well, about that last one I'm not so sure, but anyway with the others it is not so bad.

Sex is such a puzzling, intriguing thing. I don't quite know how to deal with it yet. The church says one thing, my drives say another. It's certainly not an easy thing to figure out, and it certainly isn't logical! I mean, I know all the physical aspects of it, technical names, etc., but it's the emotional part that's so hard to come to terms with.

Sex is always surrounding me, or rather my peers and me. On the one hand we are told that it is taboo, while on the other we hear "Go for it!" in our music, our dress, in our own bodies. I suppose I sound more lost and floundering than I really am. But one can become confused.

Sometimes I get so lonely. I feel so thirsty for love. I want so badly for someone to take me in their arms and hold me. I don't mean parents' love or brothers' or friends', but that deeper, more meaningful love that makes one more of a whole person. But it couldn't be just anyone. It would have to be someone whom I love very much, and they would have to feel the same for me. I couldn't compromise in a relationship like that. That's why none of my short loves have been very long. I'd always realize they weren't quite what I was looking for in a girl that got to have the privilege of being mine, ha ha. But—sometime I'll find her.

Yea!! College starts in a month. I can't wait! At last I think I'll be in my element. High school wasn't it! Not for me. I'm going to take lots of liberal arts—French, history, philosophy, writing, literature. Also swimming and fencing.

———

[At Idaho State University]

SEPTEMBER 11, 1977: [after writing about his first impressions of college life at Idaho State University, while still living at home]: The church has really been closing in on me lately. Sometimes I feel as though I'm drowning. I look at the Mormons around me; they seem content, prosperous, and happy people, but they frighten me. They're sponges, soaking up whatever they're told without giving thought to what's been said. And I hear the Bishop telling me not to reason things out, that the church must be accepted on faith. I don't know what faith is, at least in that sense. How funny. A thing that is supposed to bring joy (the church) has brought more turmoil and unhappiness into my life than anything I can think of. . . . The Mormon girls that I see at school are all the same. Granted there are the good looking ones and the sweet-spirited ones, but it's the sponge part of them that gets me. And then there are the non-Mormon girls. I like Barbara. We have more in common in our likes and interests than any girl I've ever met before but—nope, I can't really get serious with her, even though I've thought about it.

How can I explain this? None of them is deeply appealing to me. None of them! I feel little or no attraction to any of them, no matter how they're built. Jake and the other guys fall all over themselves in their panting. I think that their bark is a lot fiercer than their bite, but at least they do feel something. Mom said something like, "Well, I would suppose that you're normal and are attracted to girls?" Hmmmm—Well you see, Mom, ever since I can remember from the time I was little I've been attracted to guys. Hmmmm—Actually I fell all over myself to convince her of my "normality." I don't know. . . . How does one deal with that kind of touchy subject?

I remember around the fifth and sixth grade when Roger, Ken Martin, and I would sneak a look at the *Playboy* magazines at the super market. I knew that I was supposed to get excited and all turned on but—nothing. There was a naked woman with big boobs. So what. But I'd fake it. "Oh wow! Boy! Look at that!" I don't despise girls or hate them or dislike to touch them. The ones I know well are like my sisters. I've never kissed one on the mouth—one doesn't usually do that with sisters.

I've dated quite a lot. Some dates I enjoyed; others I could have done without. I've been attracted to some girls almost strongly, but never for long. Once in a while I feel a twinge in the loins as one walks by, but it quickly leaves. Am I gay? Perhaps. I've lived with this attraction to the masculine body, have wrestled with it, cried about it, and at times almost accepted it for so long that I'm not sure what to think. At one time when I found out what homosexuality was and that the church and "God" thought it was awful, I hoped it was only a passing phase. It's taking a long time to pass. The guilt I have felt in not being able to suppress such desires has given me some conception of what hell is sure to be like. It's not good for a twelve-year-old kid to have to carry that around on his shoulders. My parents have wondered what always made me so unhappy. How sad that I couldn't tell them. I've had this all bottled up now for eight years or so. It's not been a party.

OCTOBER 9, 1977: Since the last entry I've done a lot of thinking. Homosexuality is a subject that is difficult to say "okay" about and accept it flatly. It doesn't seem natural! I mean the idea of two men living together or just spurning women because of it. I can't believe that God intended that. There isn't anything wrong with two men having a deep affection for each other and being able to have some physical closeness between them, but there is a definite limit. I don't want homosexuality to be a part of my life. I have had urges of that kind for as long as I can remember, but it's something that I'm dealing with as well as I can. I don't understand where, at which point, it becomes evil, and how and where homosexual drives come into the plan, but still I don't want it. It's a sterile kind of relationship. One can't have offspring. It depends on looks and good body, etc., and so when one is old and flabby, that's it. Nobody wants you. How sad that kind of life would be. And most relationships of that kind don't last as long as a marriage would—I guess those that want it can have it. I still find the masculine body appealing though and feel good about that. I think that is pretty natural.

My parents and I had a long talk about sex and homosexuality a few weeks ago. Mom noticed my tripping up that time when we were talking about my "normality." She thought she had offended me, so she called me into their bedroom and we started to talk. I said I wasn't offended, but I didn't go into detail about what I wrote in my last entry either. Anyway, we had a long, open, good talk. I was surprised we could talk about such a touchy subject so easily.

Woody Allen said two things about sex that I remember: 1) "Masturbation is sex with a person I love." 2) "Bisexuality automatically increases your chances for a date on Saturday night." Maybe these are racy things to write in a journal, but I find them amusing and true. The things I write here are parts of me. I don't like the business of only writing the acceptable parts and hiding the rest. I suppose this preoccupation with sex, this obsession I could say, will cool down eventually, but in the meantime it's here.

OCTOBER 10, 1977 [after visiting a friend at Ricks College in Rexburg, Idaho]: I realized just how much Michelle means to me. I'm not in love with her. I had my times with that a few years ago, but that's long past. I think it's mutual. She's the dearest friend I have had. We relate with each other wonderfully. She is one of the most intelligent, thoughtful, devout and really good people I have met. If I could have had a sister I would have wanted her to be like Michelle. I hope my children will be able to meet her some time.

NOVEMBER 27, 1977 [remembering his recent birthday]: Also on that day I was ordained an elder [in the lay priesthood] by my father. At the time I couldn't say that the occasion was special to me, only because I—it wasn't very meaningful to me. It was a moment I had dreaded for a very long while. I feared I would be found unworthy, that the sky would fall. Also, I was not all that sure that I wanted the responsibility I felt the calling would bring. But it's over now and that brought some peace. Later I did feel good about it and proud of what had occurred.

JULY 8, 1978: The other day it rained during the afternoon. It was marvelous. The smell after it rains mixed with wet grass and sagebrush must be the most fragrant perfume in the world. I wish that I could capture it and give it to someone I love. If only there were someone.

JULY 27, 1978: I think I am in love. Oh, brother! Talk about falling for the girl next door! Barbara is looking *so* good it makes me hurt. I've gotten so I love to watch her. She's done her hair in a new permanent and is very attractive. There are many things about her (besides her body) that I like. We have so much in common and know each other so well. But I don't want to be infatuated with her. The whole situation is impossible. She was hinting tonight that I should take her out, but I don't know what kind of come-on that was: romantic or just another I'm-bored-so-let's-go-out come-on? I *do not* understand girls or women at all. I'm so naive about such relationships. I guess I'm pretty shy. In some ways I like a girl to be rather (only slightly) forward, and then I have some idea of how she feels about me. I don't trust myself to interpret subtle hints. I'm afraid I'll read them the way I want to read instead of the way intended. I know—I'm a fool.

JULY 31, 1978: Marriage is something that thoroughly frightens me. The prospect of having to be so dedicated and faithful seems impossible when I enjoy my freedom so much. Yet at times the thought of marriage is appealing. I see [Uncle] Ron and [Aunt] Adonna with their children in their noisy house and my heart warms. Other times the idea of three or four or even one crying brat chills me through. I love babies with all my soul until they cry. But I think the possibilities of teaching a child about the beauty in nature and the incredible wealth in himself would be a wonderful thing. An immense responsibility, but something I would love to do.

Sometimes I wonder how fully I should deal with my feelings concerning sex in my journal. I question what effect it could have upon someone who might read it later. Sex isn't something I'm ashamed of. I need to treat it objectively, but I do want to record how I am being affected by it.

Perhaps the main thing I'm thinking of is homosexuality. I have written only tersely on this subject in the past, and yet it has greatly influenced my life. It is something I have been dealing with in various ways for a number of years, truly for as long as I can recall. I have so many unanswered questions regarding it and heterosexual relationships.

I don't know how to cope with a desire that cannot be purged just by an act of will or because society or especially the church declares it immoral and disgusting. How easy for them to say so. I remember even as a small child watching the college frat guys who lived across from us at Riverside Park. They were always sunbathing, and I remember often wanting to go and watch them. The thought suddenly hits me: "My gosh! What are you writing this down for. This mustn't ever be known!!" But sometimes I feel as if I cannot hold it inside any longer. I must let it out.

The relationship which I long for eludes me. I don't like the idea of promiscuity, of one night stands. Sometimes I wonder if I really know what I do want. I can't say for a surety that I am gay. I guess I fall into the bisexual category, for I find the female body very appealing and beautiful, but the other seems predominant. It must be very hard for anyone who is straight to relate to these thoughts. I can understand that. There are times when I really wonder what Christ would say about this whole matter.

I am looking for something in this elusive relationship. What? A father figure? The relationships I ought to have with my brothers? I doubt it is either of those. But I feel that without it I am not yet whole. It is not possible to explain fully.

I don't like femmy guys. I myself am not femmy. I resent that stereotype and feel that it is gradually breaking down as this subject comes more into the open. I love my own masculinity. Masculinity encompasses so much more than just what is between my legs. I don't mean being macho or jockish, those pathetic attempts of some guys to prove they are men.

I wish I could meet a girl who enjoyed her femininity and being a woman as much as I enjoy being a man. This is what I want from a girl. Perhaps that really seems out of context here, but to me it isn't. Let me put it this way. Loving a guy who's relaxed about himself as a male, and loving a girl who feels that way about herself as a woman would be somewhat alike. Or does that stretch it a bit too much. Perhaps I've lost my clear train of thought—or maybe I never had it.

I could never be a gay all my life, as I think I wrote earlier. I do want to marry and raise a family. No other way could be fulfilling to me in the long run. This is confusing to me because I say to myself, "What do you expect then? A casual or even intense relationship with another guy in the next few years? Do you realize the responsibilities that entails? Do you truly want that? What about the effect on your later life?" So many questions. So many doubts. I'm rambling now. I'm not coming to any solid conclusions.

AUGUST 11, 1978: I am confused and very concerned about my relationship to the church. It's increasingly hard for me to continue to attend. It's so boring. I tell myself that I should try to find the good in the talks and discussions, but I'm tired of the endless repetition of the same themes, the same ideas. It makes me sick inside.

I'm tired of worrying about how sinful the "natural man" in me is. I'm tired of feeling ashamed of my body and feeling dirty when the word sex is mentioned. I'm tired of associating with peers who feel the same way. I'm tired of worrying about heaven when I'm not through with living yet. It sometimes seems like they want us all dead with so much incessant talk of sin and death and heaven. I'm tired of fearing a wrathful God who is always angry or pitying or weeping over me. . . .

Sex is giving me so many problems. Sometimes I feel so horny I could scream! (I'll get sued for the stuff I write in here.) Man, I don't understand sex at all. But it's stupid to say that, because I do understand it quite well. What I don't understand is how much is morally wrong. I'm just not sure any more.

I want so much to hold somebody. I want some one to love. But isn't this funny. I want physical contact so much, yet when Mom placed her hand on mine in a simple gesture the other day, I almost jerked mine away from force of habit. I had to smile. I've conditioned myself to reject such physical contact, no matter from whom and no matter how simple.

Girls become more and more appealing as the days go by, and that's frustrating. But I still keep an eye on the guys.

AUGUST 15, 1978: My parents are so good and caring. I must admit I don't envy them their job of parenting me and the others. I wish so badly that they would read what I have written in here, that they would know what I long so badly to tell them about. I'm not positive that they haven't. I don't think it would anger me to have them invade my privacy under the circumstances.

Mom asked me tonight what was bothering me, said I'd reverted to my gloomy self the past four days, that I haven't been like this since I came home from Michigan. Dad came along and expressed a similar concern. Mom made the comment that I might find them more understanding than I would have expected. We do talk so much together about so many things, and fairly candidly, but there are some things I just don't know if they could accept, or if they did accept, if they could really understand. But her comment about that, or perhaps the way she said it, makes me wonder if they have read this and know about all the confusion I feel.

I don't hide my journals. They sit out openly on my desk. I don't invite anyone to read them and for the most part expect everyone to leave them alone—honor system. Whether that has been done is the question.

AUGUST 29, 1978: I often find myself feeling that one of these mornings I'll wake up and know the secret of life, the key to my happiness. I have to laugh at myself. It's funny how strong the feeling—or perhaps the "need" for that to happen—is. I wait in a state of great anticipation. Ha! Perhaps I'll publish my findings.

SEPTEMBER 5, 1978: Dad and we older boys and [Uncle] Ron Schow went backpacking over the weekend in the Tetons. We hiked up to Alaska Basin and then down to Jenny's Lake. It was beautiful. But I am so sore I can hardly walk. I move like an old man. We had some interesting discussions while there in the mountains. We talked about science and religion, art and morals, what is sin, what is repentance. We discussed which is more important—a scientific understanding of God's works or simply a spiritual and emotional understanding. Needless to say, they were good topics and we had some interesting differing views.

SEPTEMBER 28, 1978: I go back occasionally and read over some of my earlier entries. I am surprised at how many of them relate to sex, to my feelings of frustration and many questions about it. But again tonight it is the pressing topic. For me, homosexuality has become less and less that horrible, frightening thing which it seems to so many straight people—like my father. For me it is no longer a question of evil versus good, Satan versus the plan of salvation, etc. but rather a question of a fulfilling life style. What is going to help me most to become the person and the child of God I believe I have the potential to become. For my father, the whole issue is cut and dried; there are no doubts. But people like him do not see the struggle and the variables. . . . I persist in the idea that someday I will marry a woman I love and will raise a family with her. It will be most important to me for her and my sons/daughters to understand all that I am, including that which helped to mold me. For them to know this will require that they know all aspects of my being, not just what they might prefer to know. I will never marry a woman who is incapable of understanding this part of my life and how it shaped me. But I swear that if I do marry, all thoughts of homosexuality will be put away, not hidden, not forgotten, but put away.

I have not yet met a guy who would be able to help me study and learn about this part of me. I don't know that I ever will. If and when I do in the next few years find such a friend, I am unsure just what my response will be. I am not looking for a simple fling but rather for someone who truly cares for me and I for him—or her. I want and need someone to love, to hold, to share my world with. I feel that need so acutely now.

I've told no one about these feelings. It is only here in these pages I've placed this confidence. A few of my friends might have a hunch based on our talks: if so, they have neither turned against me nor offered support. But whether they *know* is uncertain.

For me, homosexuality has the potential to be immoral and sinful, but at the same time it has, like heterosexuality, the potential to be meaningful, righteous, healthy, and fruitful if one chooses to make it so. It all depends on how it is used.

OCTOBER 11, 1978: Last night there was a show on PBS about homosexuals. I wanted to watch but was concerned about what the rest of the family would say and think. I watched it regardless. Mom walked by and overheard some of the program dialogue. She stayed awhile and watched but said nothing. When the others were finished watching the world series downstairs, I took their place and watched the rest of the show. Whether anyone was watching it upstairs I couldn't say.

I knew Mom would want to say something to me about the show today, but I knew there wouldn't be many ways to do so. She managed by just asking me what I thought of it. Dad happened by, and we were off on a discussion of that taboo subject. I couldn't believe we were saying openly the things we were saying. Dad and Mom both agreed to what they've said before about it: that it's a sterile, nonproductive sort of relationship, one in which one has to give up too many satisfying rewards available to heterosexuals— family, social life, etc.

As the discussion progressed I really pushed for my side, that homosexuality is a good thing in most cases. I had what I considered strong arguments. At one point I asked Dad what he would do or say or feel if one of his sons were gay. He said he would feel sad for us, would weep for us because of all the things we would miss. Mom asked me (I knew it would be her) in so many words if I was or could be. I thought I would die. Time to think fast. Don't say yes, don't say no, say . . . ? I don't know what I am. I told them (in so many words) that I would not run from it if the right chance came along; I made them aware that the possibility was there.

I can't believe we did it. I can't believe that I told them what I did. I can't believe that it happened. They didn't scream, yell, rant, cry, nothing. We just went on talking about it.

This is a very sketchy outline of a two-hour conversation. It was all calm and interesting to each of us, I think. I don't believe it happened. I feel only very quiet now.

It's quite ironic that later this evening we (Mom, Dad, and I) went to see Francois Truffaut's "The Man Who Loved Women." It is the story of a man obsessed with women of all kinds. He is in love with them all. It was a *good* movie.

OCTOBER 12, 1978: I feel so weary. I'm tired of always worrying about morals, God, salvation, myself, girls, guys, gays, family, school, etc. Not so much worrying but so much contemplation. I need a vacation from myself.

OCTOBER 13, 1978: Every once in a while I come down to my room, close the door, and then stand in the middle and just look around—slowly. I soak in all the things that are here. They are vital parts of me: the posters on the walls, the books which are everywhere, the antiques, the fern and other plants, the cartoons and pictures and sayings that clutter my bulletin board, the mobile of bi-planes, the spider hanging from the ceiling, the witch Mom made for me last Christmas. They all blend into what I am. They tell all about me. Someone who had never seen or heard of me before could come down here and know so much of what there is to learn about me. I find myself wanting to preserve it all, to keep it for my children to see and understand. I guess I come to look at it because it helps reassure me that I am somebody, that I am different from everyone else, that I am me. It fills me with a good feeling, with peace to come here, to be with just these things, myself, and the quiet.

NOVEMBER 5, 1978: I feel so rebellious lately. I just want out of here. Now! Nothing's stopping me but myself, but I've got to make the break soon or I go crazy! Mom says that ever since I was small I've never been satisfied with the present. I always tend to live in the past or, more so, the future. I always want to be somewhere else, and then I get there and want to be somewhere else again. Maybe she's right.

NOVEMBER 12, 1978: I do find girls attractive and sexually exciting. However, it seems to be in a different way, for different reasons. (That stands to reason, doesn't it. Ha!) But for other than obvious reasons, I mean. I watch women, girls, even very young ones as an artist would, or a photographer; I am fascinated, held by their grace and diverse beauty. I study them; I dream about them sometimes (but more often about guys). I have paintings, watercolors, photographs, drawings of them hanging in my room. But always my relationship and feelings toward them are distant, characteristic of an observer.

I find when on dates with them, I am afraid and feel somewhat intimidated. Not because they are necessarily overbearing but because I feel expected to fulfill a macho role that I have no inclination to fulfill, at least not with them. I don't think I've ever gone out with a girl I felt strongly attracted to, even though many have been good looking. Something was always missing. Women creep into my fantasies more and more lately. The other night I lay in bed "daydreaming" away, and suddenly the thought occurred to me, "My gosh, what am I becoming, some kind of heterosexual?"

Something I've begun to realize more and more is that it would be very difficult to suddenly drop a gay relationship to become a married heterosexual. I have expressed my desire before for raising a family, sharing my life with a woman I love as my wife. But up to this point I thought that it would be possible (if fate has it in store) to live with another guy in much the same way until I'm older, say late twenties, early thirties and then get married. But it wouldn't be so easy. Say I found a guy, like the one I saw last night at the movie, and we did get something going, and just say we did stay together for five or even ten years. You don't just say, "Well, goodbye,

Charlie, I'm going to start dating women now." You've grown accustomed to a life style, to living with and loving a guy, and then automatically you decide to change over to women? No sir, that won't work. And like any divorce, it would be very traumatic. That is essentially what it would be: a divorce after five or ten years of marriage. One can't do that, let alone go into a relationship with the idea of certain termination in the future. That won't work, son.

I have read some fiction in which there is a relationship between two men and a woman. The men are lovers, and the woman is well aware of the fact. She is married to one of them for the social aspects but is in love with both of them and has children by both of them. They all live in a large house on the coast of the Mediterranean. Sounds bizarre, I know. There is also a scene that I did find touching for some reason. The two men are in bed one morning having just awakened, and the children (there are three) come bounding into the room and romp with them. The children see nothing wrong with the two men in bed together or the fact that they have two daddies. Their mother comes in and the "family" talks together in the same way I remember doing with my parents when I was small.

But even as I write that, in the back of my mind I think, no Brad, it wouldn't work that way. Perhaps in books but not for real, however much you'd like it to. And then also there are concerns such as what effect such an arrangement would have on the children in their later lives and their own sexuality. It might mold them in a way that would be unfair to them. It might not do that, but the chance would always be there and couldn't be taken.

NOVEMBER 28, 1978: Homosexuality. It's such a loaded word. No— the word itself means nothing. It only takes on meaning after our minds add associations, taboos, attractions, religion, etc. It all seems so stupid to me sometimes. I think: "What's the big deal. Why get uptight about the whole matter. Shouldn't people just be able to love in a way they feel comfortable with?" More and more I think that it doesn't (shouldn't) make any difference to God or to what goes on after this life. It just all seems relative in the long run. What I mean by that is hard to explain.

For the past few weeks I've been thinking about all the negative aspects (there are many) and positive aspects (there are many here too). They seem to relate to two entirely different worlds. The conclusion I come to is that even though I may feel what I feel and be hopeful for the good in a gay relationship, the homosexual couple or single is fighting a losing battle all the way down the road.

One has several choices. You could stay independent, single, go for the one-night stands, brief relationships, and sure, maybe some excitement, maybe a lot of it. But then all you have ahead of you is to become a randy old fag who's lost his looks and nobody wants. All that is really left then are many years of loneliness. The alternative is to find a permanent lover, establish a long time relationship, settle down and share your lives together, and probably be very happy. But the problem is that very few gay relationships are able to hold together for lack of helpful glue, such as children, a socially recognized marriage, etc. But then say you do stay together in spite of this. What you have to look forward to as you grow older is still the prospect of loneliness, for you have no children, and if one of you should die there is no way to establish your rights to your mutual property because your relationship is not recognized under the law. So unless there are understanding relatives on the dead one's side, kiss it all goodbye or be prepared to drag your lifestyle into the courts.

Most straights will find it hard to accept you if you come out. You will not be able to be affectionate in public as straights are. Your relationship will always have to be hidden from most of the world. It will not enjoy the reinforcement that society offers a heterosexual relationship. To come out will change your dealings with even understanding colleagues, family members and friends. It can't help but do so.

You must always hide and live a lie. This can cause anxiety, severe depression, neurosis, etc. No wonder gay couples have a hard time staying together for any length of time. So to live, love, and be happy being gay is a long, difficult haul. It's after realizing all of that that I think, I plead: "Why should it matter? Why are people so blindly afraid?" It is in that blindness that I see the greater sin.

NOVEMBER 30, 1978: Kurt, Michelle, and I went out to dinner tonight at the Spaghetti Mill, the first time we've done anything together since Barbara left. An interesting thing happened while we were there. We were sitting eating, and I was telling them about "Swept Away," which I had seen at the SUB [Student Union Building] last night. As we were talking, I noticed a guy who looked near our age, blonde, a little heavier than me, being seated by the waitress at a table near us. He was alone. We went on with our conversation. After a few minutes we heard a voice asking what movie we were speaking of. It startled us, and on looking around I saw that it was this guy seated at his table. I laughed and told him the title. He said he hadn't seen it. I told him it was foreign and had played at the university last night. Then I turned around and resumed talking with Michelle and Kurt.

Five minutes later we were talking about a Steve Martin comedy special we'd seen on TV. Once again from the other table comes a voice saying, "I saw that show." Looking around, almost embarrassed for him, we all stared at the guy. After all, one doesn't usually interrupt another party's conversation in a restaurant. He seemed to recognize this and said something about our conversation being all he could listen to. I felt a little sorry for him, he seemed like a nice guy. I didn't know what the others would think but on an impulse I invited him to come and eat with us. Everyone seemed to relax more. Suddenly it was like we were old friends, well not quite, but it was comfortable. His name was Alan. I was impressed by his firm handshake. He was well mannered.

He told us that he was from San Francisco and that he worked for an electronics company that makes detection systems for libraries. He was up here installing one in the public library. We talked about school, about big cities, about his work, his traveling all over, about backwoods Pocatello (ha), about entertainers. It was all very pleasant.

A funny and embarrassing thing happened. The last time we ate at the Spaghetti Mill I was chewing gum, and when the meal came I didn't know what to do with it. Didn't want to put it in the ash tray where everyone would have to look at it, nor in my cloth napkin, nor on the bottom of my chair. I made a joke about putting it in the water pitcher and we all laughed. But I put it in my own water glass where it was less conspicuous and didn't bother me or anyone. Tonight the same thing happened and we laughed and again I put it in my water glass. But this was before Alan came. During the meal I was taking a drink, and he got a funny look on his face and said, "Hey, there's a dark thing floating in your glass." Oh, brother! How embarrassing. It was so funny trying to explain what it was and how it got there. We were laughing so hard, he must have thought us very strange and terribly unsophisticated. But he laughed too.

There were several things that led me to believe that he might be gay. He mentioned his girl friend more than necessary, he brought up the subject of gays as though he wanted to talk about it (this is a funny thing I find myself doing too, bringing up the subject in a casual way but also feeling the atmosphere produced and wanting to just talk with someone about it). Also he was from San Francisco, which is such a haven for gays. That fact doesn't mean he's gay, of course, but it enlarges the possibility. And then lastly, there was the way he looked at me.

There is a look in the eyes of a person who is hungry for the companionship of another person. It is a searching look, a pained look, and desire is there. It is like an animal on the prowl. It is a look that rests on the other's face and speaks a thousand words without uttering a one. It is a look that lingers just a split second too long, almost a caress, a look of pleading, a crying out for love. I know this look well, for it reaches out from my own eyes. Sometimes the eyes of two such individuals meet and lock momentarily and exchange their secret knowledge. But only if the look is mirrored in the eyes of the other. Then comes the test to see who, if either, will be strong and unafraid enough to acknowledge what he has just revealed of himself and learned of the other. I have yet to be in this position where it was acknowledged by either party. But Alan looked at me in that way, that split second too long that tells all. And I looked at him. He was good looking, but he was also intelligent and I craved that too. This look occurred not once only but many times during the meal. That's one reason I say it doesn't happen accidentally.

I couldn't have hopped into bed with him, even though I might have wanted to. I don't believe in that, but still—and even if he wasn't gay—he *symbolized* my imaginary lover. Sometimes I wonder if that lover isn't only myself.

But as we left and said goodbye, I felt bad for him, that he would be alone for the evening in some boring hotel room. We had invited him to come with us to the lecture we were going to attend at the university, but he declined, saying he had to study some of his work plans. Did he? But it was sad for us to see him get into his rented car and drive away without a friend. It hurts me too, the gay aspect aside, to know that I will never see him again. He was just a nice guy all around. Perhaps we could have been good friends.

DECEMBER 20, 1978: I'm in love with an angel. She is one of the most beautiful girls I have ever seen. She's *only* a junior in high school. Talk about robbing the cradle. She's a sister of one of Roger's friends. Her name is Trina Marsh, and she is *sexy!* I'm OK when I'm not around her, but I can't believe how she makes me feel when I see her. I always thought this melting business was bunk, but I'm proof it isn't. I feel weak at the knees, my heart pounds, and my eyes feel as if they will pop out. We went out once a couple of months ago on a blind date. It was fun, but I didn't really pay much attention at the time because I thought she was too young, probably dumb and high schooly, etc. Sure she was good looking, but so what. Now for the past month or so I've been reevaluating. Now I think maybe she's not too young, not dumb, and from what I hear, not high schooly. Anyway, I saw her at the high school choir concert Monday evening, and after much deliberation asked her to go out next week. This time you can bet I'll be paying attention.

———

[After transferring to the University of Utah]

JANUARY 6, 1979 Update: subject—sex, what else. I don't understand. I don't understand! What am I going to do about my attraction to guys? (Here comes that sick feeling again.) I like them. I can't help it. Why is it this way? I find myself attracted to women/girls only in a distant detached way. I notice their beauty and sexuality, admire and am pleased by it, but without any gut attraction. Only very seldom does that happen. The thing is, I've come to the point now where I don't really want to change. I like being this way.

JANUARY 14, 1979: I have some things to say tonight about homosexuality, and then this will be the last time that I ever again mention it in my journal. This sick feeling is going to haunt me no more. . . . Homosexuality is not a good, wholesome thing in the long run. I do not condemn experimenting with it, but any sort of long range sexuality in this area or any experimenting that would distort a healthy preoccupation with the opposite sex is very wrong!

I have had many good arguments for homosexuality. I wanted to find it OK so badly, wanted it to be logically and morally right. It had to be, because I wanted it to be. But it's not. Gradually, one by one, much to my despair, I broke down those wonderful arguments. One by one they crashed before my eyes. They had seemed so sound, so logically perfect, but they had one flaw—they just were not realistic. Their perfectness just doesn't fit the real world. I have to admit that I am grateful to my parents for being so open with me and willing to discuss the subject in the way they did, most of all for their not finding it repulsive, only non-productive, a Pyrrhic choice.

So, now it shall begin—my struggle to do not what I want to do but what I know I must and should do. I want to make plain that just because I feel this way about the matter does not mean I can readily bring this about. I must still contend with that pounding, obliterating drive, that hunger for sex. And I must still live with the layer-upon-layer effects of eight years of habitual thought. I pray to the Lord that he will help me in this. He has given me the knowledge I need, and now I must supply the determination, the guts, to move this unmovable mountain.

FEBRUARY 1, 1979: In the last entry I vowed not to write about sex, homosexuality really, anymore. But I don't know if I can do that. It's what I'm thinking of probably three-fourths of the day, every day. It's constantly on my mind.

FEBRUARY 4, 1979: My vow to never discuss homosexuality in here again was unrealistic. As little as I would like to admit it, it is very much there, good or bad, and somehow I must come to terms with it. To not be able to write about it would be to deny myself of the one outlet that I have to get the heaviness off my chest. Since I do not feel that I could openly discuss what I feel with anyone I know, this journal must lend its open, unjudging ear.

To be very honest though, I wish this journal could judge what I write once in a while. I guess what I'm looking for is complete acceptance of such a life style, someone to pat me on the back and say, "It's all right, homosexuality is not wrong. Be at peace and live as you would like." I wish my journal could do that for me. It seems that I don't want to take no for an answer.

I have met many people here. Most of them I like very much. I make friends with a few new people, and they in turn introduce me to their friends, and they again, until one knows a good number. That is how I met this guy named Edgar. A little background. He's from Puerto Rico. He's about twenty-six years old. He lived in New

York a few years before coming here. He's in the dance/ballet program. A dancer. He's about my height and weight. He also has a pierced ear and wears a diamond in it. Not so long ago that would have really bugged me. If he wasn't Puerto Rican I think it would bother me now, but that seems to make it all right for some reason.

I don't know if he is gay or not. There are not many of the usual signs pointing either way. He's not effeminate, but he moves with some grace, in a very masculine way. He moves like a dancer. I enjoy watching him. He's quite a good looking guy in his own way. He's also very hyper most of the time. He reminds me of myself in some respects.

We get along very well. I ask myself if I have some kind of crush on him. I find myself hoping that he is gay. I find myself wanting to sit down with him and tell him about everything I feel. Should I? He represents a lot of things I've wanted in my life. I like his being bilingual. He seems to be able to make his own stand on things. He dresses with a chic carelessness that I think is nice, but it is not something he seems aware of.

I think the fact that he is a dancer is the biggest thing. To me that is a mysterious world only a few are privileged to enter. He seems to be a door into that world. He and I went to the Ballet Ensemble last night. It was so good, so interesting. I felt a great contentment being there. And the fact that Edgar knew the dancers and that I even knew several of them was good too.

There was a group of mostly guys and a few girls (women) sitting on the floor in front of us watching the informal performance. From their talk and movements, they all seemed to be dancers. Some of the guys were so effeminate, masculine looking, but fems. Everything they said or did was a show for everyone around them. It turned my guts over. They were everything that I don't ever want in myself or those whom I consider good friends. But Edgar is not like that. Ballet West is putting on "Don Quixote" in two weeks and we're going to see it. I look forward to that immensely.

MARCH 9, 1979: I feel a general confusion about so many things. I just don't know what I want. Mom, Dad, and now Edgar have told me over and over just to be patient. Things will work themselves out in their own time. There is no hurrying them or worrying about when. I feel a great impatience for something. Just what I can't say. Perhaps it will always be like this, always wondering what's coming next and never being satisfied.

. . . I can say one thing—there are more gays running around here than one would ever believe (or some would want to believe). Nevertheless, I'm still not sure gay life is the life for me. I keep thinking I want something more. But what more? Children perhaps. An open relationship that needn't be hidden from the world. Things like that. Edgar says that giving such things up is the price you pay. He, for one, thinks it is worth it. I, for one, have not yet marked my ballot.

MARCH 10, 1979: I seem to vacillate between a complete acceptance of my homosexuality and then a quiet no. I have a feeling that for now it is going to be the first. I feel more and more lately that too much of a big deal is made about the subject. I'm tired of fearing myself, tired of analyzing this over and over. Straights don't have to wonder and worry constantly about why they are the way they are. They don't have to wonder about dominant mothers and submissive fathers. They don't have to worry about being condemned. They don't have to spend time in this lonely, fruitless searching through themselves. They don't have to worry whether their love is socially acceptable and whether they can show affection to their lover in public.

I think it is ironic that such a moral stigma is placed on being gay. Which is more immoral, being gay or being taught to hate yourself, to wonder always if you're not a little sick, to always be afraid. And society wonders how some gays become warped and unable to cope with the world. And then they (the world) have the gall to attribute that inability to the homosexual inclinations in the person. Which, I ask, is the greater evil?

In the past I have looked at the subject through others' eyes. My parents have had the greatest influence. Most everyone else made little difference. I found that Mom and Dad's logic was sound. Their advice seemed convincing. But for all their understanding and openness, they do not know what it is like to want it so bad. I like guys. It's been that way for as long as I can remember. For whatever reason, whoever made me this way, however it happened, psychological, biological, social, sick or healthy, it makes no difference in the long run: I am what I am. . . .

I feel good about myself and what I am. But even as I say that the wheels inside my head begin to work. Are you really? Are you just saying that because you'd like it to be true? How do you know you are? Could you really be happy being gay? Where did you become this way anyway? Was it something you ate? Did your mother do this to you, or maybe your father? But if you are gay, when did it start? What about not having a family? What about promiscuity? Are you just running away from reality? Are you afraid of girls? Are you in love with yourself? What about loneliness? How will you cope with that? Do you really think that guy sitting next to you is so good looking, or have you just gotten into the habit of looking at guys instead of girls, a habit that needs to be broken? And so on.

"I wanted only to live in accord with the promptings which came from my true self. Why was that so hard?" —Hermann Hesse (Demian)

APRIL 27, 1979: "Nothing is more difficult than not being one's self or than only being one's self so far and no further." —Paul Valery

JUNE 29,1979: The things which have taken place in the past month have had a great impact on my life and have caused changes, directing my course into new channels. First, there was my trip to New York. The city has given me a taste of a life I crave. I will return there soon.

Second, there is my relationship with Jon. It grows and develops every day. We are together all the time. The possibilities for us are wonderful. I love him and need him so much. I've never felt like this about anyone before.

Third, I told my parents last weekend about my being gay. It's out and done at last. It was very hard for them, very upsetting for me also. They now know about Jon. I know now that my relationship with my parents will never be the same. I've crossed a bridge that will never be open to me again.

My father says that he will be surprised if my homosexuality lasts longer than ten years. He feels that I just reenforced one of two possibilities and that time will show me the other is more fulfilling. He does not deny its reality in me but feels it is probably only a subconscious backlash against parental and church authority, a need and desire to identify with a group, also partly the excitement of identifying with a persecuted minority. Perhaps. I don't really care why it's there anymore. For whatever reason, it is there, and I'm trying to adjust my life to it.

Just when I felt I was beginning to be comfortable and happy about my sexuality, my parents turn it over and help bring back the old anxiety about it. I know they do it because they love me and must deal according to their own insights which become increasingly different from mine, but I must say they didn't help me at all. That was why I told them, to get help and guidance. It only made things worse. Still, I'm glad I did it. All things considered, they took it quite well. But I am so confused and have nowhere to turn for direction.

———

[Living in Los Angeles]

SEPTEMBER 23, 1979: I am living in Los Angeles with Jon. We have been here since the beginning of September. He applied for a fellowship at USC sometime last year and got one of the appointments. . . . He made it known to me at the start of our relationship that he would likely be leaving Salt Lake for southern California at the end of the summer. We wondered what would happen to us if that did occur. . . . Summer arrived and wore on. Our relationship grew and deepened. I moved in with him about a month after I came back from New York. It was more convenient, and it was nice living together, but I didn't really unpack my things because we were unsure what the end of summer would bring.

We could feel the tension. What were we going to do? Jon wanted me to move with him. I wanted to, felt excitement and joy at the thought, and yet I wondered how I would explain it to my family and friends. I was torn. I have neither time nor inclination to try to describe how hard a period it was. . . .

When Jon left to find a place in L.A., I moved into another apartment alone. Mom and Dad came down for a visit one weekend, and we discussed the situation candidly. They asked me at last what I planned to do, would I leave or not? It was at that moment I made the leap and said, yes, I'm going.

And so here I am. That's a very sketchy outline of what has happened and doesn't begin to do justice to the complexity. But let me say that against everyone's advice, family and friends and also my own better judgment, I moved down here and I'm proud that at last I had the guts to make my own decision. I feel very good about it. Jon's and my relationship is suffering through the adjustment of the move, new city, new jobs, etc. I'm sure he has had as many second thoughts about us and this arrangement as I have. But that goes off in another direction.

My family has given me nothing but the best support since I made my decision. My parents, needless to say, are worried and not altogether pleased with the move or the situation, but they have begun the long process of trying and perhaps beginning to understand. I'm grateful to them.

Roger found out about my sexual preferences also. He took it quite well. He too is not pleased but perhaps will learn to be accepting. It has drawn us closer together. We have become true brothers since he found out. I'm glad he knows.

JULY 8, 1981: Several years now since I have written down anything. Many, many changes. Almost a new life—a whole new person. So much more on the way, however. Anyway—it's time to get back into the habit. As for what has passed, I'm afraid what is gone is gone and I doubt that I'll try to recapture it here. Bits and pieces perhaps.

I'm now living by myself in a still unfurnished apartment and feel a sense of true satisfaction. *I'm on my own.* I am changing constantly, and at last I think I'm prepared to deal with it all.

JULY 15, 1981: I went to a screening of *Rainbirds* tonight with Brad and Renee. She is an up and coming Dutch film actress whom we met last year. The screening was at Fox. The movie was OK. . . . It was at once interesting and exciting and horribly dull to be back at a screening with the same old crowd of people. All the people Brad and I met when he was working for Dan Ireland. It was good to be back out with Brad again. I still love him. We go so well together. We both enjoyed it. Old times all over again.

But it was the same false scene. Fawn and cry over everyone there and praise the picture to those in charge and the stars and then leave and dish everyone and tear the film apart. The banal comments! Brad was outdoing himself tonight. That is the Hollywood I intensely dislike. But it's the glitter and the show that give it excitement.

I miss Brad. There were times when we were so happy together. Living on Detroit Street . . . for almost a year. We were so in love. And our Orange Cat. The Rabbit VW with the incredible tape deck. Climbing up the back stairs high as kites at five o'clock in the morning and dropping into our huge bed and wrapping our arms around each other and falling asleep.

JULY 21, 1981: I had a pretty good day. Got up at seven, read in my book on stocks, cooked a good breakfast. Crossed off several of the notes on my job list for the day and went to work.

Stuck work out all day! I'm proud of myself. It was a struggle.

The work is MINDLESS! It's not even a discipline problem any-more. But I need the cash. I stuck it out. Good for me. Points, points. I need to pat myself on the back as much as possible for progress and high spirits.

I've got to get away from that law firm job, do something different. I want to start my own business, a gardening service. I would gain a vast amount of knowledge and discipline from such an experience. A lot of planning involved, but I could handle it.

NOVEMBER 23, 1981: I've got to find some sort of creative outlet. My runaway libido has got to be brought back home again—if it ever was there in the first place. Somehow I've got to find an escape from this semi-depression I'm submerged in. I feel like my life has little meaning, no purpose. I find myself searching for a lover, but that is not the answer. My new part-time job at the Pottery Barn is about the most satisfying thing in my life now. It seems good to be back in the retail environment and to be working around functional things. They are delightful to my eye and help nurse my battered sense of self. I need some new goals. Money seems so tight right now. I cannot get ahead financially, and I feel that I am fairly frugal. In any case, I do need that artistic outlet.

DECEMBER 10, 1981: Bored. It seems like everyone is bored. Let's find another kick. I'm living in a town full of jaded, desperate people. Need to escape. There has to be more. But you can't go home again. Once you've tasted this, your thirst will never be quenched. Doomed to feed on myself and this town even though I realize it will eventually consume me, or bury me in its wake.

FEBRUARY 3, 1982 [speaking in the third person]: Just out of a hot bath, he lay on the bed sweating. Fighting to identify the classical music on the radio—was it Vivaldi? He cursed his neighbor for the steady, low disco beat that assaulted him through their shared wall.

He mused on the fact that he was flying home to see his family the next day. A short visit, only three days, but perhaps even that would be too long. In ways he resented the idea of losing an otherwise perfectly good weekend. He cherished those few free days. He disliked anyone impinging upon that time, even though he rarely used it to accomplish anything productive. Perhaps it would be nice after all to see the family again.

But these visits often turned out to be harrowing emotional experiences, dredging up old childhood anger, reducing his self-confidence, renewing old doubts, turning up unpleasant memories of guilt and self-hatred.

He stopped there. It was Vivaldi. He shut off the music and the light and slept.

MARCH 12, 1982: *"If you can't find it where you're standing, where do you expect to wander in search of it?"* 50 pushups done.

MARCH 21, 1982: L.A. crouches like a beast outside my door. She sits on my front step, beckoning with a long finger, saying, "Come on, there's a party going on, and you are invited."

It's hard to sit home. Sometimes I feel like a caged animal. I don't know whether it's because the apartment is small or what, but it seems a prison that I have to get away from. There are times when I enjoy it. I run out of things to do here by myself. Reading is about the only thing that I can turn to. The TV's broken. I find I'm sleeping a lot.

I have to learn to be a calmer person. I have to learn not to worry so much about things that cannot be changed immediately. I have got to learn to be satisfied with the now. I've got to learn to be easier on others *and* myself. I'm not doing badly, all things considered. But here there is so much pressure, so much stimulation, so much materialism. One can totally indulge in hedonism here. "Let's go consume," as Scott would say.

MAY 12, 1982: The whites of my eyes have the color of yellowed ivory keys on an old piano.

MAY 15, 1982: I went to the doctor today. He told me that he doesn't think I have hepatitis. He said that apparently I have a flu virus that has irritated my liver. I'll take his word for it. It felt lousy to think I had hepatitis again. To me it is an illness that signifies uncleanness or excessive partying and drug use. I have not been guilty of these. That was why it was so demoralizing. . . .

Living in a big city kills the ability to sit still. Relaxation is a difficult art.

MAY 17, 1982: The gods came and spoke to him while he was in bed with a high fever. He couldn't get any sleep because they all wanted to talk at once. His dreams were closer to nightmares, a constant barrage of voices; like watching ten TV channels at the same time.

JULY 12, 1982: I don't understand being gay. Sometimes I feel like I was cast in the wrong movie.

AUGUST 4, 1982: I think at times that L.A. must be the coolest city on earth. But it's like too much cocaine. It gets to the point where you need more and more of it to get you off, and I don't feel like I'm getting high any more. So many unhappy people. So much frustration, so much pressure to live the illusion of a life of wealth and status—to be ONE OF THE BEAUTIFUL PEOPLE, man!

"People are too concerned with whether they're going to appear cool, or hip, or whether their 'street' credibility will suffer if they do this or that. No one's going to be hip forever. Who cares. The important thing is to follow your instincts, and produce the best movie you can." —*Joe Jackson*

——

[In Hawaii]

SEPTEMBER 26, 1982: The gods talked to him constantly, ten TV sets blaring at once. He wondered if he was just a bit mad and would slowly become more so. Since they all talked at once he couldn't understand any of them. Very frustrating to be talked to by not just one god but ten! And not be able to hear properly. . . .

The journal began to be less and less a record of personal events and emotions and more a playpen of random thoughts that needed no logic or purpose. An alter ego taking on a personality of its own, a schizophrenic outlet. . . .

Hawaii was beginning to bore him. Not being able to find a job or an apartment in two months was becoming depressing. He felt sometimes that the island was rejecting him.

There were some consolations. His lover was beautiful, the pout of the lips irresistible. There were miles of tropical beaches. But otherwise he felt stagnated. What was he doing here?

JANUARY 10, 1983: I lost my job today. No warning. Only a message not to come in. Depression, a feeling of inadequacy. A prison of boredom—again. Why can't I just be an artist. A life that is streamlined. Mine has so many snags.

"Nobody is allowed to fail within a two-mile radius of the Beverley Hills Hotel." —Gore Vidal

———

[Going back to Idaho]

FEBRUARY 13, 1983: I'm leaving Hawaii. Going back to Idaho for a while and maybe to Sacramento later in spring or summer to work for Brent. Hopefully school, landscape architecture, in the fall.

Hawaii has been good, a nice transition. Why am I so insecure about my decisions and my life thus far? My moralistic self wants to brand me and have me suffer for the past few years. I'm suffering from this backlash. I'm losing friends as a result of my moralistic judgments; am becoming increasingly schizophrenic, paralyzed by my harsh, puritanical, hateful side which confronts my lustful, blundering but progressive self. I have to keep it all in control. I hope going home helps and doesn't hinder. I know that I'm trying really hard. Please don't let everything I've loved so far be a mistake, as it seems in their eyes. I can handle it.

MAY 3, 1983: I've almost finished a second month of my Babylonian captivity, in other words, I'm still in Idaho. Being here dredges up all sorts of memories, many of them unpleasant: old feelings of guilt (that prison without walls); adolescent emotions from high school which amaze me in that they can still twist me around the same as before, emotions of inadequacy, lack of confidence, the need to measure up to the old macho creed. Just walking around these streets brings the boogies back. And then there's the inescapable dark hand of the church. This too surprises me, for I had forgotten how much suppressed anger, frustration, and hatred can accompany one who dares to be independent.

Living at home is both a cradle and a curse. On the one hand, it's nice to be back among these people with whom I grew up and have shared so much, to feel a part of a unit, to be needed by *my* family, to draw *some* strength from them. And yet I find myself retreating back into some of my old adolescent patterns of suppressed anger and frustration in my relationship with my parents as I am temporarily dependent on them. They have given me great leeway to do as I want, and yet I still—perhaps only in my mind—feel the subtle pressures, and my own anxiety over our differences, and the need to *prove* myself in their eyes.

In ways, I almost feel like an anthropologist on a mission to study the nuclear family from within. I feel both attached and curiously removed from them, as though I had never seen them before. In some ways I really hadn't. It's difficult to be objective about something you've not broken with yet, as a child not having any basis for comparison. The question is, "Do I really like these people?" a question which I wouldn't have dreamed of asking at one time. The answer, by the way, is yes. Blood is thicker than water.

Still I feel, perhaps because of my age or perhaps because of my sexual orientation, the urge to go far away from them. I feel that somehow I don't quite fit. A square peg in the proverbial round hole. And also I feel sad about my inability to communicate, or their inability to understand, what it really means to be gay, that flame that burns in my soul. I am beginning to despair that they will ever

understand, accept yes, understand no. A source of great hurt for
me. By not understanding, they—who could be my most delightful
and satisfying companions—are separated in spirit from me. Without meaning to be tragic, I think I have no choice but to go away,
to seal off the hurt with distance and occasional phone calls. Perhaps
this will change with time.

JULY 13, 1983: I realize intuitively (and at times through conscious
deliberation) that happiness, long term happiness, is not going to
be gained by life in the fast lane, by a constant pursuit of transient
pleasure, which is what my few years in Los Angeles so largely
consisted of. Anything else seemed to be a bother, to be standing
in the way of the "earnest" and "real." Thus I spent a lot of time (and
still do) feeling dissatisfied because life gets in the way; i.e., I don't
have much money, I have to work for a living, I can't be in two
places at once, I have to go back to school, etc. I could make a long
list.

The vision of life I was shown in L.A., or perhaps the vision I
saw because of my own predilections and fantasies, was one of
endless sensation, a kind of movie world, a fantastic realm where
things are always "too cool." Such a world, however, also seemed
to be constantly evasive, just beyond my fingertips. This was much
the case for most of my L.A. friends also, none of us having been
born with a silver spoon in our mouth, yet we ached for and, yes,
at times felt we had attained that idyllic moment. But it *always*
seemed to finish too quickly. What a crash, what a disappointment.
"You mean I'm not one of the beautiful people?" Cinderella at 12:00
midnight. Back to the ashpit, back to the struggle, the endless
frustrating pursuit.

Somehow I want to reconnect with the real world. Life isn't the
fantasy I wanted it to be. In looking back, already I'm beginning to
see how *young* I was. To go through all that would be hard on
anybody. I've a few battle scars to show for it.

*"But I was in search of love in those days, and I went full of curiosity
and the faint, unrecognized apprehension that here, at last, I should find*

that low door in the wall, which others, I knew, had found before me,
which opened on an enclosed and enchanted garden, which was some-
where, not overlooked by any window, in the heart of that grey city."
—Brideshead Revisited

JULY 28, 1983: My days sometimes seem to pass in a dream-like
state. I move from the pools of my unconscious dream world of
sleep and go swimming at the gym shortly after waking up. The
sensation I feel—to have moved so quickly from the one liquid
reality to the other—is strange. It can become difficult to discern
whether I am really awake and swimming with a sense of having
been previously sleeping, or vice versa, sleeping while dreaming of
moving in this cavernous liquid womb. From the pool I go sit in
the steam room, sometimes for nearly an hour. Again, here is an
"unreality," a small oblong room, very warm and humid, the steam
making the enclosure seem possibly much bigger, a womb again.
Images continue to flood forward, mind trips. Home to study; all
day spent with my nose in a book. This seems to be but a
continuation with somewhat more direction. The day is one long
flowing mental river.

JULY 29, 1983: I miss homosexual company. I miss being able to
share fully the sense of irony that our lifestyle brings with it. There
is no one here who understands. I have tried and tried to explain
to my parents the fundamental differences in sensibility between
homosexuals and straights, and yet, as I do not fully understand
them myself, I can only fumble and search for words which fail to
express this thing. Philosophy, outlook, value system: all these
words and others fall short of that spirit which makes GAY. Indeed
it is something of a spirit, perhaps a muse which touches some and
not others. I end such discussions feeling total frustration and,
sometimes, unspoken anger. But I am beginning to realize that such
things do not need to be explained to everyone, even if it were
possible. My necessity for explanation comes from my own need to
understand and defend. As I grow more comfortable with myself,

I suspect that much of this need to explain to others will die away.
. . .

Two years since I began this notebook. Bits and snatches of a
wild time in Oz. ("Is there life after Oz, Glinda?") A new phase has
begun in my life. I'm growing up, slowly but surely, and yet at times
I feel as if I shall never grow old, remaining one of the Lost Boys
forever.

Facing the future is frightening. I try to project my mind forward
to divine hidden events, but can only guess at possible scenarios.
Being comfortable with the unknown is not one of my strong points,
nor is living in the present. I suppose the future will be here all too
soon.

SEPTEMBER 26, 1983: Reading Hesse's *Demian*. Very interesting. I
have always seen myself in the characters of his novels. The same
again this time. It is as if he had read my thoughts before they or I
existed. The books always seem so relevant to my needs at the times
I have been reading them.

———

[At Utah State University]

OCTOBER 2, 1983: So classes have begun. One week gone by already. This thing is not going to be any easy task. They are working
our butts off. I suspect they enjoy their own tyranny. The whole
thing feels like some sort of initiation ceremony into a brotherhood.
If you pass the test (the final at the end of the second year), you've
made it into the club, you've proven your worth. Well, I want to be
in their club, I tell you, and they can throw their worst at me. I'll
give it my best shot.

OCTOBER 14, 1983: Living in this community throws my oddness,
my homosexuality into sharp relief. It seems impossible to blend
in, to be a part, to think like the people of this community, this
mentality. A sad story.

OCTOBER 15, 1983: Mom and Dad stopped by tonight on their way back from Salt Lake. They had said they might, but still it was a pleasant surprise. I took them over to see the department studios where I spend so much time. We got into a discussion in the sophomore studio about the light and dark sides (Apollonian versus Dionysian) of one's personality, I saying that I love the dark side, the danger of falling, Mom saying that she is frightened for me.

I have to laugh at us, the way we drop into such deep and intense discussions at any time. How typical. Was so good to see them. We went and got ice cream. Their 26th anniversary tomorrow.

NOVEMBER 16, 1983: There are the good days and the bad ones. On the bad ones I feel as if I'm falling down a dark hole, grabbing at the sides with my finger nails, trying to hold on. Or I feel as if I'm crawling, slowly, blindly, groping my way through the hours I have to remain conscious, wishing and waiting only for the time when I can find some respite in sleep.

The good days are marked only by the lack of this darkness moving in over the horizon, much like storm clouds which I am powerless to stop, able only to watch their approach. The good days are only characterized by the lack of this unbelievable numbness and fear. The last week has been pretty good in this sense, if one can call such a feeling good.

NOVEMBER 20, 1983: When I reread my entries from the past few weeks/months, it seems hard to believe that I can get so low at times, that things can be so bad. The problem is that they do and often put me at my wit's end. I'm bored here. There are just no two ways about it. I don't know what to do.

In trying to be positive about the whole situation, I can say that Logan is beautiful (as it always has been). The program here is definitely a good one—probably one of the best. But other than that I am at a loss for any other good words. I feel as if I am living my life in a vacuum—no friends, no real stimulating conversation, no night life, no confidante, nowhere to get away. Have I made a gross mistake in deciding to go to school here? Should I have gone back to California and tried to study there—Davis maybe?

DECEMBER 4, 1983: I've been in one of my anti-homosexual moods again today. Raging inside myself against the horrible anti-social sexual werewolves that we all are. Right? Like I said—what's a boy to do? I have to confess, I don't understand the whole thing. Is it symptomatic of other more deep-seated problems? Am I rebelling against the world? Am I afraid of growing up and refusing to accept responsibility and my own mortality? I long for love, but do I really know how to love, or is it just neurotic projection of my fantasies. But when I think about living the rest of my life with a man (not mattering that we "might" love each other) I am hit with a wave of straight homophobia.

DECEMBER 6, 1983: As I have said before, the common life here in this small, rural, middle-class town contrasts powerfully with the life that the majority around me (and even I at times) see as abnormal, the homosexual life. I think about how much safer and more at ease I felt living in the ghetto where there was security in numbers, where you weren't constantly reminded of your "oddness." (That is, until you got off the bus—with fifteen other men who all looked, dressed and acted the same and went to the same places.) Perhaps I deceive myself into thinking it was much more comfortable there. Self-destructiveness certainly existed at a peak level in the ghetto. Even though we were all comfortable with our "gayness," we seemed hellbent on doing some damage to ourselves, whatever the consequences. That isn't comfort.

JANUARY 19, 1984: I'm enjoying my classes so much. This is what keeps me going. Design, Graphics/Sketching, and Site Analysis. Just finished a design problem for Dick Toth. Composition showing enclosure/implied line w/ focal point/balance, etc. Fun but I feel drained. Worked all day to finish by 5:30. Very pleased. Don't know how the grading will go. Must write about my attitudes toward this man and why I like his classes, why I hang on his words—and hope for his respect.

JANUARY 20, 1984: Went to a party tonight, with a girl from class, Monica, and her boyfriend/lover, Paulo. Both from Argentina. Fun party, with quite an international cast—South Americans, Europeans, blacks, a few Orientals. I had thought this type "scene" did not exist here. There is life in Logan after all.

NOVEMBER 1, 1984: I try to approach my stay here as a sort of Buddhist test. Now is the time when I must learn control: control of my desire/hunger, control of my self-identity, control over that raging animal which tears at my inside and seems close to breaking free. . . . There are too many times that I feel my grasp, my ability to pass the test turning into a failure. It seems to be more than I can deal with.

I need to turn my anger and fear into physical activity, to work myself to the point of exhaustion so I don't carry such poisonous flammable material around in my head. If I cannot find others to share with me, I will do it myself. I will beat it out of my own hide! *But it must not be done in anger.* I need some sort of daily workout. I have to begin to press myself in this area, into a new direction.

FEBRUARY 6, 1985: I have been reading a book on Buddhist thought and tradition. I'm enjoying it very much. It echoes so many of my own ideas about the world and the painfulness of life. But it says that we can break the chain of birth-sorrow-death-rebirth by *right action.* I believe this is true. I feel it innately. I think I have always known it. This is my way out, most likely not in this life, because I am too addicted to the sensual world, but possibly in one soon following. I feel that little by little I am moving in that direction . . . .

Talked to Mom on the phone tonight. She sounds so calm it's almost unreal. She has found her peace at last, much as my father promised she would. Much as he has promised that I will also. I long for mine, and I feel happy for and envy Mom. My parents are certainly my closest friends, perhaps that I will ever have.

MARCH 9, 1985: Hung out with some of the local gay flora tonight. I felt like a third thumb. There were four of us. . . . My discomfort was *not* of my own making. These guys all reminded me of so many of the queens that used to be in the bars. Sort of super faggot types. I think my anger is stemming from my loneliness. There's that word once again. Isn't there anyone around fairly normal *and* gay? The two aren't necessarily mutually exclusive. What am I doing here? Why can't I meet people whom I'm comfortable with? Where are the people like Scott and Richard?

APRIL 14, 1985: My homosexuality has always put a damper on my confidence. It has made me hang back from the others in games and anything that included an element of physical aggression. It has helped create, along with the melancholia, a very introspective life, a sort of pale, sickly child of the mind.

It may be that my attempts to make friends have been awkward. They have, granted, often involved a sexual attraction on my part, and therefore have made me into the shy, gawky kid. But then there have been very few people I really wanted to know. I long for people like Chris with whom I could discuss literature, art, philosophy, etc. at a stimulating level. Scott understands music and aesthetics, although he knows nothing about literature. Richard, also, could relate to philosophy, and at bottom I just plain enjoy his company. And so I ask myself why it has been so difficult to find such people here. I realize that these three friends were gleaned from a great crowd of people I have met in the last few years, and I did not meet them all at the same time. Making good friends is not a quick process. Brian today made me feel a greater interest in him and his ideas than I have felt for anyone I've met here . . . .

But once again in my friendship with Brian, who is so very heterosexual, since he knows nothing about my homosexuality, he knows nothing about a great deal of my life. It is the crucial part of the puzzle. He cannot know me and understand my thought and experience without it. It becomes like trying to tell a story and having to leave out key elements. Great gaping holes. And because

I am afraid of his reaction to such a revelation, I stumble on trying to avoid making the gaps apparent. Such a fear can become quite a blockade to true friendship.

APRIL 17, 1985: This tape makes me long for Los Angeles. Living there was such great fun. L.A. and I were made for each other. I wonder how I can even consider living elsewhere, including San Francisco. I can't believe that I'm in Logan. The very idea is oppressive to me. I feel almost obsessed with the idea of getting out of here, whatever the cost. I must have been crazy to think I could ever be happy to spend four years here. But I can remember the rejection mentality I was in at the time I made the decision to come, feeling that I had to renounce the "fast life" of the big city and in no small way "punish" myself for having been such a promiscuous and highliving bad boy. And so we move to the opposite self-denying extreme of the spectrum. If I have learned anything by coming here, it might be to try to be more moderate in my choices. Happiness is not to be found by bouncing between the two poles.

MAY 15, 1985: I have wanted to write about this for a long time. But I have felt too ashamed about the fact that I "cruise" in the gym dressing room. Certainly my cruising is not blatant. In fact, it may be that I don't pick up anyone because they can't tell I'm even interested. I find the whole business sort of dreadful. What an odd thing to be writing about. I don't think that anyone who is not gay could understand this matter. I sometimes think about how it would be for a heterosexual man, like my brothers or my father, say, to be able somehow to move freely among the naked bodies of women in their dressing room, without the women being aware of it, of course. He would blend in with them and yet would be like a wolf in sheep's clothing. This is my situation. I am a wolf among the sheep. Like a predator in the steamroom, patiently waiting.

Last night for the first time in a long while I thought how foreign is the thought of living the rest of my life with a man. It's fine in romantic fantasies but more difficult in reality. I have become more attracted to women in the past couple of years. I look forward to the time when I fall in love with a woman and sleep with her. I think about children more all the time. I long for domesticity in my life. I think about big houses and grandchildren and the type of environment I would like to provide my children for growing up. I think I would make a very good father and partner. Ideally, what I seem to be longing for at this point is some sort of menage-a-trois, with another man and a woman. How the logistics would be worked out is uncertain. I have fantasies about meeting a man, falling in love, and on my telling him of my desire to meet a beautiful woman to marry and have children with, one who would understand my homosexuality, he would introduce me to his sister. A woman could also introduce me to her brother. But it seems important that they be tied together in some such manner.

I am homosexual. There is no doubt about this. I feel that this is now and will always be my true nature and inclination. But my aesthetic appreciation for women is developing and expanding into a more sexual inclination. I am beginning to feel a need for a female presence in my life, for a counter-balance that only a woman could provide.

———

[Again in Pocatello]

JANUARY 1, 1986: I have been intending to write for many weeks now. This seems an appropriate day to get around to it finally. [He recounts briefly the events leading up to his November hospital sojourn in the intensive care unit.] Not a pleasant experience. More info can be obtained from the other members of the family. I don't remember too many details about the whole thing, thank goodness. Since then I have been on the slow road to recovery. My health is much improved. I feel like a different person. (Perhaps I am.)

Mike has gotten engaged to his girlfriend Marnice. I have to admit that I'm kind of excited by the whole thing. Someone from outside coming into our family.

It's the new year and I have several goals I hope to fulfill:

1. I want to learn to juggle. I made myself some blocks filled with beans, made them today on the sewing machine. No small feat in itself.
2. I want to start learning some magic/sleight-of-hand tricks. I have wanted to do this for some time.
3. I want to learn to play my harmonica. I have wanted to do this for a long time too.
4. I want to write with more regularity. Several times a week if possible.
5. I want to start playing the piano again, eventually resume taking lessons.

These are simple things. I seem to have a great deal of time for them on my hands, but it is a commodity that may be in short supply.

FEBRUARY 8, 1986: There are times when I feel so restless I could just scream and scream. Absolutely everything seems to irritate me. But at this point there really isn't much I can do about it. Mom made a comment today, that I might have to stay here for a very long time because of my illness. NOT IF I CAN HELP IT! This WILL NOT be my fate, to live out my life in Pocatello.

Now when I sit down to write out all the things I've been thinking about the past few days, everything turns to sand and slips away. I need to eat something. I feel sick from not having eaten enough today.

FEBRUARY 17, 1986: The doctor gave me the results of some blood tests today. They are basically unchanged from what they were in the beginning of my illness. My system is still screwed up. This is disappointing. I had been entertaining some hope that because I've been pretty healthy lately, perhaps the virus was dying. Apparently

not. But being discouraged will not help. I should continue to be thankful for the health I'm experiencing right now and not be concerned with what might go down in the future. I will not worry.
. . .

Still, I can't help being bummed about the results of the blood tests. I want to live! I want to get better. I have been making plans. Wasting away was not one of them. But get a grip. One never knows what fate has in store. Before I got sick with pneumonia I didn't have much desire to get better and very little desire to live. I just didn't care. My mental state was *very* bad. Something changed in the hospital. I was offered a choice: to go or to stay. It was up to me at that point. I made the decision to stay. I have been approaching life with renewed vigor, finding enjoyment in things that had become empty for me earlier, like music and reading. Now that I am involved in living again I feel afraid of death in a way I wasn't afraid before. I have too much at stake, too much to leave easily, things I want to do. I have to stay well. At some point they're going to find a cure.

I have been swimming with some regularity the last few weeks. I am surprised at my new found strength, though I can't go as far and as long as I could before my illness. But it's getting better, a good sign.

There are about ten old men that have been swimming regularly at the gym for years. Watching them is like watching the March of the Troll Brigade. Some of them wear flippers on their feet. They sit in the steam room with me after their swim. They do "exercises" in the steam. Waving their arms about, lifting their legs as they lie on the slab table in the middle of the room, they look for all the world like plucked chickens, their skin hanging, their withered breasts sagging above their bellies. Lord knows if these "exercises" help much. But the effort seems to satisfy the old men. Eventually they shuffle out slowly, their knarly, grotesque feet looking not quite human. I've been wanting to write about the old men for some time now.

FEBRUARY 23, 1986: I think Mom is as bored as I am. Some nights we two alone end up parked in front of the TV, aimlessly switching channels. We hand the channel changer back and forth, as if by letting someone else do it something of interest (even slight) will appear out of the wasteland. We both need to get out of here, out of this town, off this planet. I think I've watched every nature show ever devised.

My walk yesterday was so pleasant in spite of the drabness of the weather. I keep thinking about it. It was wonderful to be outside again. And I had a great swim today. Many laps, no fatigue. There was a pregnant woman in the pool today using a kickboard to paddle. She was graceful like a sea cow or manatee is graceful. Very nice. As I swam I could see only her legs and belly beneath the surface, this big extended orb. She was quite pregnant. I wonder if—and hope—her baby will like the water as I do because of this early exposure.

FEBRUARY 24, 1986: There are times like now where I'm sitting out in the warm sunshine reading my book when I think, "I could possibly die soon, but I have stayed alive long enough to enjoy this moment." I'm glad for this. I don't mean to sound sappy. I saw a butterfly today, the first. Maybe that's sappy. But a good sign.

MARCH 30, 1986: *"One day you're here and that's fine, and the next day you're gone and that's fine too, and someone has that very day come in to take your place whatever that might have been."* —City of Night

APRIL 14, 1986: Listening to *Der Rosenkavalier*. It makes me want to cry. The thought flashed by again today (it doesn't happen too often) that I am not ready to die. I want to live. I want more. *I am not done yet.* I still have to keep my appointment with that mysterious lover in my dreams. He's out there waiting for me and I refuse to believe that mysterious person is only death.

APRIL 21, 1986: Early morning. I have spent my life up to this point believing if I searched long enough that life and the "way" would reveal themselves to me, that my sheer desire would squeeze it out of the clouds and ether. This obviously has not happened. I am quickly coming to the point where I realize that the answer to my questions is, there are no answers. This is it. Some actor said something about this life not being a dress rehearsal. "But isn't there something more?" I am so restless. I want to throw plates at the wall.

Evening. *"A man of old has said: 'Those who practice meditation seeking things on the outside are all imbeciles.' If you make yourself master in all circumstances, any place you stand will be the true one. In whatever environment you find yourself, you cannot be changed."* —The Buddhist Tradition

APRIL 22, 1986: I have not felt good the last few days. I'm feverish most of the time, similar to the way I felt every day before I went into the hospital. This is only a recent development.

It rained hard today. Was beautiful. Everything is very green. Tulips everywhere, but no daffodils. Beautiful tulips, more than I've ever seen.

I feel discouraged because of my illness. It's left me in this weird limboland. I feel like a prisoner and wonder if this is how it will be from now on. Some days I've felt that I could easily work full time, or at least hold a part-time job, but then on days like yesterday when I feel like crap I know there's no way I could hold a job. And so I'm becoming an invalid, trapped in my parents' house.

MAY 10, 1986: Many things—I just watched a show on the Shakers and their community and beliefs. It made me want to cry (I've been emotional again lately). Their lifestyle was so simple. They achieved such serenity and peace in their lives. All things they did, they felt they did for God, and so they tried to do all things well and with pride. Their lives were celibate, and this in turn gave them great creative energy. They believed in equality and love for all men.

Contrast this life to that in F. Scott Fitzgerald's *The Beautiful and the Damned*, which I just read, where people are only concerned with materialism, temporary beauty, and are cynical, oh so cynical. It made me feel awful because I recognized in it much of myself and my years in Los Angeles. I felt sick inside.

I have long thought of becoming a monk of *some sort*, withdrawing from the world into a life of work and contemplation. Somehow I have to find my way back to my god. I have yearned for this and hurt for this for so long.

On the one hand, celibacy seems so desirable. For me anyway. I am so tossed and whipped by my desire at times it seems impossible to deal or live with it. I feel I have become a slave of that of which I ought to be the master. And yet I believe and know that sexuality can be a wonderful, God-given gift.

AUGUST 13, 1986: *"He would go on a journey. Not far—not all the way to the tigers . . . three or four weeks of lotus-eating . . . in the lovely south . . ."* —Death in Venice

Looking back over my journal, I realize that a great change in my attitude concerning my illness and my imminent death has taken place over the last few months. As it has become apparent since those entries that dying soon is my fate, I have spent such a lot of time (I had little else to do) thinking of death and preparing for it that I have come to hunger for its release. The thought that it could be denied me for now, that I could go into remission again petrifies me. I ache now to be released from this life. The waiting seems unbearable and cruel at times.

I am worn out physically. Some days I can hardly move from my bed for lack of strength. My weight has dropped far from the return to 140 during spring to 120. My appetite is poor, and I look very thin. My hair is also coming out like it did when I was so ill before. I show all the symptoms that I displayed before I had to go into the hospital except the daily fevers. It is my hope that by September or October I'll be gone. I am so tired of this.

SEPTEMBER 5, 1986: Thoughts—Scott's here. Arrived this afternoon. Many effects—on self, family. Good to see him.

Feel more in control. Situation will not run me anymore. Making more effort with family to be less defensive, less caustic, and quit playing old games. Decided to transcend somehow. Scott here for a few days only. Last time to see him. Have to be careful not to be caustic with him also. His importance to me is beyond measure. How will I be without him? My eyes keep closing—tired. Listening to Rachmaninoff ("Isle of the Dead"), Debussey. Favorites. I feel ambivalent about death again. Yet I am so tired of this. Family has been very weird lately. So wonderful to have Scott here.

Being home destroys any confidence I have gained. My parents are *never* wrong.

I'm going to die soon—nothing to do about it. I miss Genesee [the street where he lived in L.A.]. That was a cosmic point for me. It goes with me in my heart. I can't describe it. *Personal*. Scott would know.

OCTOBER 22, 1986: Further adventures—My illness is progressing nicely. I have lost my ability to be mobile on my own. I hardly have the strength to get out of bed and my legs have atrophied. There is talk and a lot of thought about the need for canes and wheelchairs. I'm losing the peripheral sight in my left eye and find myself surprised that this bothers me so little. My appetite is good—maintaining weight between 110 and 115. I have been sleeping literally all day and most of the night. Socially I have withdrawn from everything. I feel ambivalent about having my California friends call for news and would be content never to hear from them again. (Writing is becoming difficult. I feel spastic.)

Got a card from Joyce Parsons today. Really fine to hear from her. Nice to know that my feelings of affection for her and fond memories are still reciprocated. Must admit I was a bit surprised.

Listening to Firebird. Top ten. I'm losing it. Can't concentrate anymore. Have to stop.

III. Letters to Brad

In January 1979, when Brad left home for the University of Utah, we began corresponding. That June he revealed his sexual identity to his mother and me. In the early fall he moved from Salt Lake City to Los Angeles, where he lived for a little more than three years. He then spent several months in Hawaii.

The distances that separated us during those four years were in some ways a metaphor for the distance in our relationship. Though there was no definitive break between him and us, his move away from conformity, his search for new values, and his decision to embrace his sexual orientation softened the ground that separated us, made it boggy and difficult to negotiate. He needed space in which to work out his self-definition. We recognized that. He felt stiff with us, not surprisingly since our resistance was unmistakable; we were diffident about intruding when it might be unwelcome, when it might be misunderstood. There was, I am convinced, a desire on both his part and ours to overcome this strain, to get comfortable with one another again, but it was more easily desired than accomplished.

One result of this was that our contacts with him were less frequent than I might have wished. He came home once or twice a year, and we visited him in Los Angeles twice. The telephone was our easiest means of connection, probably once every three or four weeks. He wrote fewer letters than we did, but we did not overburden the postman.

As it turned out, Brad saved the letters we wrote him during those four years. They were left among his few belongings when he died. Most of my letters to him were follow-ups to telephone conversations, my attempts to give a more enduring, and therefore a potentially more influential, form to my arguments about values. That he saved these letters tells me something, though I know his ties to the past were becoming less relevant at the time.

I have recently reread them. They reveal a great deal about family tensions of the period, about issues that concerned us, about ideological jockeying for position on his part and mine as he went about the business of attempting to create an authentic self and as I tried to exert a father's influence on that process according to my agenda.

I reread them now with considerable ambivalence. They reinvoke for me the sense that Brad was attempting to navigate treacherous waters and that I needed to share my experience with him. At the same time I am chagrined to recognize the limits of what I then knew outside the boundaries of liberal religious orthodoxy. I confess that as a result my advice was sometimes flawed. I acknowledge that my good intentions were not always helpful.

Both Brad and I in some ways assumed I knew more than I did. He wanted to trust his own experience where it contradicted my advice, but he was intimidated by the veneer of sophistication in which my opinions were packaged. I failed to recognize that the world offers a wider range of legitimate personal possibilities than I had grasped, and that I too was involved in a process of broadening my philosophy.

And yet that is not wholly accurate either. For there is some evidence in the letters that on one level at least I did acknowledge my need to participate in a genuine dialogue. Over and over I declared to him my intent to approach him as an open-minded friend. Because I cared for him I would willingly hear and weigh his truth. I think I was sincere in these expressions. But both of us had a hard time forgetting the built-in power distribution in our father-son relationship.

I realize now that these letters are problematic texts. They demonstrate the contradictions inherent in the prison house of language through which we attempt to understand the experience of others and ourselves. On the surface they contain a father's well-meant counsel, the best advice he was able to give at the time. But they are filled with subtexts that run counter to the explicit statements.

These contradictions—indicative of complexity in the situation and the relationship—can be decoded by a careful reader. For example, the text states repeatedly: "I am not now a domineering father, I am your friend; I don't want to make authoritarian negative judgments about your experience." Subtext: "Nevertheless, I have much more experience than you, I am demonstrating that by what I write, and here is what I think you should be thinking and doing." The text reads: "If you must be homosexually active, find a worthy long-term companion and be monogamous." Subtext: "I don't even like the thought of your living with another man, and therefore I'll not be available to meet your lover, not here nor in L.A., not now and likely not in the future." And again, the text reads: "I want to accept you as you really are." Subtext: "You'd better be prepared to *prove* that identity. Moreover, your asserted sexual orientation is so repugnant to me that I can hardly bring myself to say the 'H' word; thus my written style is characterized by all sorts of delicate verbal avoidance and indirection."

Such subtexts weren't there by conscious intention. But I see them now, and I am convinced Brad recognized them at the time.

I try to give myself the benefit of the doubt. I remind myself that I cared very much about what was happening in Brad's life—not altogether selfishly—and that I wrote letters with his best interests in mind. Nevertheless, as I reread them, I keep hearing echoes of Shakespeare's Polonius, Laertes's pontifical father. Besides serving up a generous portion of platitudes, my advice was at times simply wrongheaded. For example, when I said things like "This step has, inevitably, enormous consequences for your future life," it sounds like a philosophy of fear. I should have lightened up a little. That might have helped him to do the same and to see his life as a natural process of trial, error, correction, growth; it might have helped him look more optimistically at his future possibilities. Instead, with my gravity I weighted him down.

Not the least Polonian aspect of my stance was the sense that he was racing ahead of me in his development, that I was trying desperately to catch up and influence what had already occurred. And weren't my attempts at diplomacy too transparent and condescending? And didn't he know that? I did so much want to be his friend, but did I instead rob him of self-confidence?

What I present here are excerpts from the letters, specifically those parts that bear on Brad's situation and our dialogue about values. I omit informal small talk, family developments, local news and weather, comments on books, films, politics, etc. Although their omission makes the letters seem more formal, such matters are not germane here.

———

17 February 1979

Dear Brad—

We were glad to get your last letter. As your mother read it to me on the phone, I smiled at your poetic description of your butterfly-chasing propensities and said to myself once more: "Yes, he is undoubtedly a romantic." In *Lord Jim*, Stein, an old Dutch trader in the Far East, says the same thing about Jim—and he was right. Sometime you will have to read that book.

Romantic temperament has its positive dimensions; it is idealistic, rebellious, individualistic, intense, glamorously impractical, emotional. It has also its disadvantages: egocentrism, constant unrest, unpredictability, disregard of objective realities. The romantic is a paradox: he is both superior and limited.

I know something about this temperament because I have a bit of it in myself, though I cover it from others' notice pretty well. This strain of my personality was stronger when I was your age. On the other hand, of course, I have a good deal of the practical "mensch" in me, the side you are more familiar with—the rational, even-keeled, cool-headed part of me.

So do you. You are not a *pure* romantic but a mixture. It is useful to recognize that. The trick for people "like us" is to acknowledge both sides of our dual natures, and to maximize the advantages of both while minimizing their disadvantages. To do this is to move away from extreme romantic behavior, of course; it is also to forego cold, unimaginative pragmatism. One needs to avoid the roller coaster ride between extremes, keeping some practicality, some self-discipline while also nourishing a certain amount of idealism, intense feeling, sensitivity, and healthy individualism.

I didn't mean for this to sound like a lecture or even *heavy* advice. And in calling you a romantic I intended to pay a compliment. These facts about my life may give you some familial perspective on your own. So look out the window at your butterflies, admire their beauty, chase them on Saturday afternoon for the fun of it. But for the rest of the time, keep focused on your practical affairs. Interestingly, romantic goals can *sometimes* be realized—but if that happens it is usually because the person pursued the dream by means of disciplined strategies. A nice paradox, eh! . . .

Stay well, stay productive, stay happy. Dad

———

Sunday, June 24, 1979

My Dear Son,

Though I said that your declaration did not come as a complete surprise to us, still we both find that after all we are not, were not, emotionally prepared. You must understand that this requires a radical reorientation of thought about many things, for it is inevitably, inextricably tied to so much—in the past, the present, and obviously the future. This awareness has been with you for some years now, and it has taken you this long to come to your present vantage point. You must be understanding, then, if we require some time to come to terms with a phenomenon we do not entirely understand, especially since it involves the renunciation (quite possibly) of some of our fondest hopes. I say this at the outset because it seems to me that we did not measure up to your hopes of us as you declared your situation. You wanted, clearly, that we should understand the matter in all its complexity as you presently do, that we should accept what you now consider to be your course, that we should not cling to the possibility of other explanations, of the possibility of a future change given further experience. You wanted us not to urge *our* old values and *our* doubts on you, for that only makes things harder for you. Isn't that so? Perhaps you went away questioning, if not our love for you, at least our intelligence, wondering if we lacked the courage to face facts, wondering if after all we don't still mean to exert our subtle tyranny over you.

I am sorry that we could not, after all, entertain your friend. To have done so would have reassured you and been demonstration of marvelous broadmindedness on our part. But surely in retrospect you can see that was expecting too much too fast. It is one thing to bring us to a confrontation of the likelihood of your homosexuality; it is yet another big step to ask us to evaluate a man whom you are considering as a lifelong companion. You see, don't you, how very, very difficult that would be to handle with equanimity in the space of forty-eight hours. Nevertheless, I would like so much to feel that you went away from us strengthened rather than frustrated, and I'm afraid that was not the case.

You may be wondering at this point if, after all, it was the best thing to have told us. Well, do not have any second thoughts on that—it was best that we should know. If there is pain involved for us, certainly there has been pain for you for a long time—and will probably continue to be in some degree. If love between us means anything, to me it means sharing this fact together. Our lives are bound together in ways which cannot be undone, and if our relationship is to have real meaning, it must not flinch from such a test. To be in a family implies ideally that we support each other in the best way we can (perhaps even by resisting), and that cannot happen in ignorance.

As you know, I read the long letter-essay that originated at BYU [i.e., *Prologue*], and your mother is well along in her reading of it. I have also done a little reading at the university library and plan to do more. At this point it seems that no one pretends to have full knowledge of the phenomenon of homosexuality and its causes. But I did see several books (recent studies) which say there is a continuum in sexual responses, that the disposition of people is not into two wholly separate camps, that bisexuality is possible, with varying degrees of commitment to either side, etc. At this point I assume that you feel sure of where you stand on this continuum, but I am not confident that you have certain knowledge of all your options or your emotional and sexual possibilities. You will say, do say, that your experience with girls to now has convinced you that your basic inclination is not toward them: I would argue the possibility, at least, that your teenage experience did not adequately, fairly test your sexual compatibility with women. How much sexual experience with girls did you have, after all? You always complained that they hadn't enough intellect—but then how many of your male teenage friends did you find intellectually stimulating? It is probably too soon to conclude reasonably that females cannot provide adequate intellectual stimulation for you—there are very bright ones around, in fact.

Perhaps, as the BYU letter writer argues, one does not choose his sexual proclivity; still how to respond to it as a given does involve some choices. Yesterday in Soda Springs I observed a young woman with her child, and it reminded me powerfully of what a pleasure it was to be very close to your mother as you and the other boys were prenatally formed, as you were born, and as you grew up with us. Pleasure is not an adequate word—it was to observe something very beautiful at close hand, intimately. It was to have a modest part in a wonderful creative process, to know through that cumulative experience perhaps the truest joy of my life. It is very sad for me to think of your missing that, particularly if you need not miss it.

But, you will say, "You are trying to impose your values on me, you aren't willing to grant me freely the right to choose my own course. Furthermore, I don't want the hassle and responsibility of children." OK. But do you really know your own mind on these points just now? Many young men don't. I'll give you a specific case, Harry Donaghy, who as you know was a priest until past thirty when he decided that he very much wanted children, a family. And now the delight he takes in Nora and Marty is clearly visible whenever he is around them. Don't put such experience out of reach prematurely. It is still too early. You are in college, a period when one is bombarded with new and heady doctrines, philosophies, ideas. So many persons have vacillated hither and thither in the midst of this stimulating growing experience, only to see certain old values gradually reemerge in their lives and thought. "But," you will say, "my sexual inclination has long been clear." And I say—perhaps. But can you just now absolutely know where determined sexuality ends and other social, intellectual sympathies begin—or vice versa? When I spoke the other day of homosexuality being a kind of religion for you at this point, perhaps I was not kind. Still you seemed to agree. If that is so, it suggests that you may in fact be dealing with a preference which is more intellectual-psychological (and thus changeable) than psychological-genetic. *May*, I say, for I do not know. My question is still, do you know absolutely? Probably not. Wouldn't it be wise then to be cautious?

I am proud of you for many of the things you said in our

two talks during your visit—that you are determined at all costs to avoid promiscuity, a homosexuality that has its *raison d'etre* in superficial sensuality, that you are preparing yourself to be a real contributor in an enduring relationship, that you are committed to proceeding very carefully and very slowly. I pray you will not waver in that resolve. In a situation such as you find yourself in, where the risks are even greater than in the process leading to heterosexual marriage, and especially when your own goals and desires *may* be less than fully clear, a chaste homosexuality would still be the wisest possible course. A friend of the type who could be a fine long-term companion will be willing to wait until you have had sufficient time to be sure. "How long must I wait, Dad?" you said, and perhaps not very kindly I replied: "Until thirty." Well, there is no magic number, but you can afford a couple more years at least of intelligent "cruising" among both sexes. Give each side its day in court; you haven't done so yet, though I think you've tried. But teenage experience is not a sufficient trial. You have so much more to offer now, and so does a potential female partner. "I don't plan to date," you say. OK, don't date. But do you *date* homosexual friends? Do *see* females who are intellectually stimulating to you, explore your common interests and share some good times with them. Who knows, perhaps you'll even come to want to *date*.

When you left and I said we'd be praying for you, you said that was irrelevant but to go ahead if we derived any comfort from it, words to that effect. I don't think you understood me quite. We will not pray that you be necessarily "changed," but that light and understanding and strength and courage will be yours (and ours) and that you may find a way to a happy and rewarding future. I don't pray too much in conventional ways, but I believe that the world is permeated by divine spirit and that we can put ourselves into harmony with it. I believe that others through faith and seeking can influence our lives positively in this way. If I were you, I'd look for some of that divine guidance on my own, and I would not discount the value of the sincere prayers of others on my behalf. Let us hear from you.

Your loving father

━━━

13 July 1979

Dear Brad,

It was good to speak with you the other night. I'm glad you called us back. It goes without saying, I suppose, that you have been in our thoughts almost continuously since you were home. On the more mundane level we have been wondering about whether you would find an adequate apartment and job; more significantly we review over and over what you told us, trying to interpret it, trying to gauge its implications for the present and the future. Personally, I can come to no settled state of mind about it, my assessment vacillating from day to day. Of one thing, however, I do feel convinced, that it would be a mistake for you on the basis of your present position to conclude confidently that your future must necessarily deviate from the more conventional patterns of sexual relationship. Of one other thing I am sure, that your mother and I want to be as supportive as we can, helpful, understanding, loving friends who desire only your present and future happiness, friends who will respect your individuality while at the same time holding up a mirror to some things which you may not see. I am hopeful that we can talk again about these matters—if you wish to. But I will try to avoid intrusion if it is unwelcome.

You will see that I have included a book for you [*Surprised By Joy*]. I know that you have admired some things by C. S. Lewis, and I find that he can always be read with profit. This spiritual autobiography is one I have just discovered and appreciated. So many of Lewis' youthful sympathies and experiences reminded me of yours that I felt you would enjoy a kindred spirit's account. You will see, among other things, that he values greatly intellectual male friendships, that he too has found relatively few very close friends. I will be interested to learn what you think of the book. . . .

Dad

---

4 February 1980

Dear Brad,

. . . Apropos of the moral vision in *Garp* [by John Irving], I'm not particularly impressed. It is more defensive than positive or affirmative. It is a response to the gothic and grotesque elements in life; and while the grotesque and the gothic certainly exist, one needn't allow them to dictate the terms of one's existence. Acts do acquire moral significance by virtue of the human dimension in them, but that doesn't need to mean total relativism or arbitrariness. I reject a morality where one chooses anything he wants and justifies it as OK. If some religions have been narrow in their moral creeds, that is no argument in favor of an equally untenable chaos. Rather, the discovery of narrowness should impel one to pursue a holistic view of morality, one that seeks to perceive all the subtle implications of a moral choice and to act responsibly in accordance with that broad, intelligent perception. The moral philosophy of Jesus Christ, as I perceive it, is not narrow but rather encourages the fullest, most sensitive response from us. To see it as restrictive in a negative sense is to have bought someone else's bill of goods, not Jesus'. I'm not sure I understand in what it is you have felt cheated, but I can't believe that *real* Christianity, *real* Christian ethics are responsible.

Nor do I quite agree that all religious systems are intended to hold man in subjectivity, insuring their survival by instilling in him the need for what they proclaim (isn't that the essence of your statement?). They may, of course, degenerate to that. But man's need for morality is part of his nature, I think, necessary for his spiritual well-being. Consider the analogy of weightlessness in space: it may be a lark for a while, but before too long one yearns for something firm to push against. Only within a physical environment where something solid exists to thrust against can one's action be decisive, effective, meaningful. Similarly, we need—each of us—the equivalent in the moral-ethical realm, something to push against, and so it is in our nature to seek moral certainties, firm places. I believe they exist, but we must find them with holistic, responsible vision.

Well, this is too complicated a topic to be handled in a single page, but I did feel inclined to respond to your brief comments—which I may not have understood. Wish we could have a long relaxed talk about this. . . .

Love, Dad

—

22 May 1980

Dear Brad,

. . . And how are things with you, my friend? Your change of address and change of roommate come as a bit of a surprise and naturally leave us with many questions. What happened with Jon? What kind of person is your new roommate? What is the nature of your relationship with him? And, of course, all of the questions which bear on evaluating your situation at present. You have obviously come to the end of a chapter, one that must inevitably have enormous consequences for your life. I am wondering if you would not be wise at this point to give yourself a breathing space before you embark on another intimate homosexual relationship, time to get some perspective on where you are and where you want to be going. Obviously, I am hoping that the new roommate is not more to you than a friend and someone to share expenses. More than that would be unseemly haste.

Even as I write this, I am conscious that once again I may be intruding as a heavy parent, trying to exert a dominating influence.

Well, I don't want that, don't want to deprive you of the right to live your life. But I feel that I want to be your friend. I hope you'll regard my comments as indicating the best kind of interest, concern, and love rather than as intrusive and insensitive meddling.

Perhaps a homosexual life is what you will finally opt for, in spite of its difficulties. But in my mind at least, there is still some possibility that you could find a satisfying heterosexual life. (Have you seriously considered counseling?) And I am still convinced that in the world of real relationships, your chances of achieving a stable, happy, productive life will be far greater if you can find a female companion and are willing to help make a good marriage. There is much to be said for having some degree of stability in your life. A series of twelve-month, or short-term, relationships will keep you off-stride unceasingly, unable to settle down. There is just too much biologically and socially that militates against happy long-term male homosexual relationships.

At this point you have not gone too far to turn back. You have tried the homosexual life and you have lived in the homosexual ambience. Undoubtedly you will say you learned from it—but that is quite possibly because you had to make sacrifices and compromises in living with another person, not because of the homosexual dimension per se. Do you see what I mean? You have time to be patient. You've opened one present before Christmas: now settle back and don't be in a big hurry. You might just decide you want to look for the presents under a different kind of tree. As Conrad points out in "The Heart of Darkness," many men get smashed on the rocks because they are not capable of restraint. Whatever your choice may be eventually, you'd do well to cultivate restraint just now.

As for the uncertainty about getting back into school, I don't know how to read that. Is it that your private life is unstable and so emotionally absorbing that you can't concentrate? Is it just that you don't have a certain career goal? Is it that you can't handle the financial problems associated with getting back into school? Perhaps you just don't care about "formal learning." But lack of restraint and stability may have some bearing on the matter.

Brad, you and I both know that you have a keen mind, one that can benefit from more rigorous mental discipline. A good liberal arts education continued on the present foundation will be ever so valuable to you, aside from the question of careers. Maybe you'll end up wanting more than just four years, but at least when you get that B.A. you won't have to hesitate about searching for, applying for jobs that have a future, because not only will you have a better trained mind, you'll have a recognized credential. So why wait to get on with it? Set your goal, then if there are obstructions, find ways to get around them. As for being a waiter, that's OK if it's a means to an end, like getting ahead so you can go to college again. But not just so you can work less. Work more! Get two jobs if necessary! It will do wonders toward relieving ennui, and it will make you positively *glad* to get back to school.

Well, this may give you something to grind your teeth about—or to think about. Whatever your reaction, these thoughts are at least well-intended on my part. . . .

Love, Dad

———

Sunday, 24 August 1980

Dear Brad,

. . . Ron and I had some good talks while we were hiking, about God and our relation to Him, about goals for middle-aged types like us; and we talked some about you. Ron seems to be quite openminded about homosexuality, that is, he is convinced that it isn't well understood, that the jury is still out on some aspects of it. Certainly he feels that many people are unchristian in their response to homosexuals. I think he doesn't consider it the best way to go if one has any choice in the matter, but he acknowledges the possibility that one may not. His concern for you just now was that you may be in an environment that is not desirable in terms of your total development. He raised the question of the kind of friends you may have, not necessarily whether they are homo- or heterosexual, but what kind of values they may have otherwise in the larger scheme of things. It was an interesting question for someone like me who is greatly interested in your happiness and welfare. It causes me to think of those areas that Socrates spoke of as essential in our lives—the good, the true, and the beautiful. Or call them ethics, knowledge, and aesthetics, if you will. I think you should reflect on the implications of these facets in your life, particularly consider the tension that exists between the ethical and the aesthetic. I think the richest life comes as a result of keeping these in an appropriate balance, and I think if there is a tendency in your life just now, it would be to be vulnerable to the aesthetic life, to the exclusion of the ethical. Don't misunderstand me; I don't mean to suggest that you are hedonistic or lacking in principles, etc., but you are certainly living in an environment which leans very heavily toward the aesthetic orientation. I am speaking not particularly of the gay community, about which I am not well informed (though I know that many in that subculture are primarily aesthetically oriented) but about the kind of attitudes that are widely prevalent in the free lifestyles of southern California. I can't develop this very satisfactorily in a one-sided letter conversation, but it's something for you to think about. How *are* your friends and acquaintances oriented? What really matters to them? Are they the kind who will stick with you when things go a little awry? Are they durable? What do they stand for in terms of building and preserving culture? Do their basic values square with yours? This is not the heavy father but the friendly, loving father speaking to a son whom he very much respects. Perhaps sometime in the near future we'll have an opportunity to talk of these things in person, and if you are interested I can refer you to Matthew Arnold, Thomas Mann, Thomas Carlyle, Plato, and others who were interested too in these matters. . . .

Love, Dad

P.S. I do need to know what you want done with your church membership records. Can't you send the name of your friendly neighborhood ward? Then you can establish whatever kind of relationship or nonrelationship with them you wish. If it is a problem for you, it is nonetheless one for which *you* should take the responsibility.

———

26 October 1980

Dear Brad,

Well, it's been a week since you interrupted with your most welcome phone call just as I wrote the date on this page. . . . Again, thanks for the letter you wrote us. I delight in your awakened interest in the many facets of life around you and in their interrelationship. That your experience in L.A. has stimulated your desire to learn, to gain basic practical knowledge is all to the good. Remember that completing your college education is only a part of the process. Much of what you want to learn can be (and ought to be) learned informally through private reading and discussion and activity. You mentioned having fallen into the habit of sleeping excessively. That doesn't sound consistent with the thirst for growth you described in your letter. I expect it was temporary, but you could use 2 or 3 or 4 extra hours daily to very good advantage. The things you want to accomplish are worthy, but they require some organization and some discipline. Read Benjamin Franklin's *Autobiography*. We can all learn something from him in that respect.

I was interested in what you wrote about ethics and moral obligation. That is a very complex and important subject. One can't be fully human without having worked out some kind of ethical position. Certainly there are differences of opinion about what ethical behavior involves, and it would be surprising if you and I or anyone were to agree on every particular of what is moral and ethical. Thus I understand what you mean, I think, when you wonder if *my* ethics is entirely relevant in *your* situation. But at the same time there is a bedrock of ethical principles on which I hope you and I agree, including the following: the golden rule, honesty and fairness in dealing with others, respect for others' rights, respect for life, willingness to contribute one's share to the common good, etc. If your evolving ethical philosophy doesn't embrace these, then I'm concerned for you. But I feel pretty confident that regardless of our differing experience we'll continue to accept these basics. I would enjoy some extended discussion of this subject with you when we can (indeed, it's a subject I enjoy discussing with just about anyone). . . .

Much love, Dad

—

9 April 1981

Dear Brad,

There is a lull in the action at this State Board meeting which will give me time to write a few thoughts to you. We were glad to talk with you the other evening, though I must confess that the substance of your call, that is, your decision not to continue with school, came as a considerable surprise to me. I believe it was that element of surprise more than anything else that left me somewhat vague in my response. "The readiness is all," says Hamlet at one point, and it seems that what you were trying to tell us is just that the moment is not ripe for you to be at the university now. No one is more convinced than I that pursuing a course at the university is frustrating and almost pointless if you are doing so without enthusiasm, if your heart isn't in it, if the work seems unrelated to your life or your future goals. You can only force it to a certain degree; beyond that it doesn't work. I have seen more than a few students in just your state of mind—and have seen the difference in them and their work when they returned after a few years with an honest motivation originating in their own desires, not in family or social expectation. I know too, of course, that many able, determined individuals have succeeded in life—professionally and personally—without a college degree; a degree is not a *sine qua non*. When one reads John Henry Newman's classic treatise, *The Idea of a University*, a liberal arts education seems like a highly broadening, tempering experience; unfortunately many college degree recipients don't have that kind of education anyway—they just get practical training—and job training in some kinds of work you can get elsewhere.

You are the one most in touch with your life, your goals. And you have time (I remember that my own college experience occurred largely after I was married—ages 23-26, 28-32). So don't feel pressured to do what is not "ready." I suspect sometime in the future you'll feel an *inner* urge to do some more college work. When that happens, if it does—and it might be twenty years from now—you'll find satisfaction in it along with the hard, sometimes frustrating work. But please don't ever feel you have to do it for the people you know in Idaho. If you never go back and you are happy with the results of that decision, it is certainly all right by me.

Parents try to advise their offspring in terms of choosing paths that are *in general* most likely to lead to satisfying outcomes. But what is good in general may not be good *specifically*. You are now an adult and able to make good decisions for yourself. Perhaps it will be for you as it is for some, you'll bounce around, progressing by trial and error rather than moving straight towards your goal. Well, such learning is part of life. College learning *can* be very good for some people, it can have good effects—in general. But it is *only* in the general sense that we encouraged you along those lines. I'm sure you see what I mean. I really hope you know that "my goal" for you (a misleading phrase) is not that you should be made in my image. And I hope you know that I have confidence in your ability to plan intelligently for *your* future. After all, it *is* yours to plan and live.

I was sorry to learn how you feel about coming home. I hope it is not because you feel you have to defend your life against criticism from us. And I hope you know that our love for you and our concern for you are not conditioned by or qualified by "where" you are now. Maybe the problem is that you feel some ambivalence in yourself between the old life here and your new life in California—and coming home is apt to stir up that tension. If that is the difficulty, I guess you'll just have to resolve it yourself, and that may take some time. Years perhaps? I hope we won't have to wait that long to see you. In any case, I hope your problem with coming home is not due to your not being able to respect and appreciate any longer our values and the way of life here.

April 20: Have just read the paragraph above and have a different thought about it: relax about the coming home business. Don't make a bigger deal of it than it deserves. If you expect trauma, the expectation will probably be self-fulfilling. Accentuate the positive, as the song says. . . .

We think of you often and send our love. Dad

———

12 July 1981

Dear Brad,

. . . Apropos of my trip to L.A., I still have extremely positive feelings about it. You were a very fine host/guide, and I enjoyed simply everything we did and saw. But most of all I was glad to revitalize our relationship as close friends. I am glad to have learned some of the things you taught me; I sincerely feel that my perspective was broadened by several degrees—and in more ways than one. I would be glad if you were to feel similarly benefitted by our dialogue, which I found challenging and enjoyable. I had begun to forget how much we have in common aesthetically and intellectually.

It is exciting to see someone (like you) intensely engaged in the business of self-discovery, self-definition. Though it is a struggle at times, the kind of conscious quest you are involved in can be—on the whole—so rewarding. I came home convinced that you are making good progress in your effort to find authenticity. I found you developing your sensitivities on many fronts, and I rejoice to find that you are cultivating your ethical sensibilities as much as anything else. I want you to know that I do believe in you, that I have faith in your ability to find authenticity and a meaningful future, that I am proud of you. You have great challenges ahead of you, and though you are taking some risks, I think you will manage to stay in control. But I do not think anyone is invulnerable. It does not seem smart to me to prolong risk-taking indefinitely when the learning or benefits involved begin to decline.

I was much impressed with what you had to say about mind/mental control of one's life, relationships, health, etc. I believe you are right in asserting that a person can have enormous influence on his own "destiny," his own course of development. One of the reasons I believe strongly in your future is that *you* believe in it and are determined to make it fruitful. You are facing a number of practical problems—financial and social—and you must make important education and career choices. Regard these not as obstacles but as opportunities. I am confident you can find solutions and can handle the occasional frustrations that go along with choosing not-the-easiest path. . . .

Apropos of your coming home for a visit: I still think it is important that you do it this summer, and I trust you remain of a similar persuasion. One of the most important things I gained from my visit was the example of the Boyd family [an extended family, observed at a 4th of July picnic, which showed comfortable and loving acceptance of a gay son and his friends]. Through them I now know—not just intellectually but on a deep emotional level—that the relationship of a gay family member like you to the greater family can be close and rewarding for all—including your brothers' eventual wives. So it is essential that we continue to cultivate our knowledge and understanding of each other in person as much as possible. . . .

Love, Dad

▬

21 November 1981

Dear Brad,

Just a quick note this afternoon, mainly to say hello and let you know we are thinking of you. Particularly as the Thanksgiving holiday approaches and we will be getting together with the Schow clan in Preston, we'll miss you. I do hope that you will be with friends you enjoy and that you will have something like a traditional meal to feast on. . . .

In this season of Thanksgiving, one of the blessings I am most grateful for is that you are my son. I love you deeply, and I feel you have much to offer me and others. It seems to me that you have a fine future ahead of you; I feel hopeful and optimistic for you. Your route may not be the most direct one to your goals, but you will get there. From my point of view, our relationship is now moving into a very rewarding phase, partly because your self-growth enables you to perceive me differently, no longer as a domineering force but as a caring, supportive friend. We will always be father and son to each other, but I hope in the most positive sense of that relationship.

Have a happy Thanksgiving. Dad

▬   .

19 May 1982

Dear Brad,

The semester is over, grades are in, commencement past—and now I can take a little time to put the details of my life—academic and private—back into order. So I've made a long list of such things to attend to, and sending this note is at the top.

You'll find enclosed the story by Andre Gide ["The Prodigal Son"] that I mentioned to you. When I read it, I was deeply moved, for much in it seemed to parallel your experience and the various possible responses that in one degree or another have followed. I am sure you will see that the story can be read symbolically—and I am also confident that you will agree with me that the people and situations in it are not exactly analogous to the circumstances in our family. You will, I'm sure, find Gide deeply perceptive, deeply sympathetic, and extraordinarily honest about the nature of individual experience. I think you are aware that Gide himself was homosexual. He was indeed a great writer. Perhaps you would enjoy reading other things by him, for example "The Pastoral Symphony," a short novella.

In "The Prodigal Son," the religious establishment is symbolically presented and its limitations revealed. In thinking about your experience, one of the sad and disappointing things for your mother and me—and doubtless for you—is that the church, which ought to have provided help and understanding to you, was incapable of it. You did not leave the church so much as it left you. . . .

Just one thought as I close. When we last spoke on the phone, you said your self-esteem was—for the moment at least—dragging. Well, I just want to remind you to keep some perspective on things. Seems to me you're doing very well in some important ways. Seems to me you're taking charge of your life very responsibly, digging yourself out of a bit of a financial hole—that won't take you too long, and in the meanwhile you seem to be learning about other rewarding, relatively inexpensive, long-term pursuits. That's not bad at all. 23 years is, after all, still an early age. Anyone who makes you feel that you need to have arrived by 25 or 30 or even 35 is a fool. Consider my case—I went back to school at age 28, stayed at it four years, didn't complete my dissertation until I was 35. Don't let the worldliness of the L.A. life blind you to the fact that you are unique, have your own rhythm, your own pace, your own values, your own way. Have patience! Keep your own counsel, stay attuned to your own feelings, your own inner voice—and of course keep your intelligence awake and your antennae out. (I know you are doing that.) Time and patience, my son. In the meanwhile, think well of Brad. He's a fine young man with a promising future. Remember that you have our love—and our respect as well.

Dad

———

16 June 1982

Dear Brad,

I have been thinking a good deal about our recent telephone conversation. After such a talk, one is always mindful (or should be) of the inherent difficulties in interpersonal communications: is what you said and meant really what we heard and understood—and vice versa? That I do not fully see your situation as it appears from your perspective is a given—each individual's perception is to some degree subjective and cannot be entirely shared by another. Bearing this in mind, I nevertheless want to comment on several things we talked about, and their implications. My intent is not to lean on you heavily in paternal fashion but to share my views with you as a friend, one whose perspective may well be worth considering, one who cares deeply about your happiness and well being.

To be frank, Brad, I see you getting more deeply into a situation, the dangers of which I am becoming increasingly aware, the dangers of which you appear to be at least nominally aware but which you dismiss somewhat fatalistically. I am not speaking of homosexuality per se. Notwithstanding the social difficulties it entails, I believe it possible for homosexual preference to be compatible with a healthy life, both physically and psychologically. I am no longer hung up on that point, and I think you know that.

Rather, I am thinking of the grave dangers to physical and mental health posed by certain extreme dimensions often associated with gay life style—the health problems associated with sexual promiscuity. This applies in both sexes of course, but now, for reasons unknown, especially among gays. The hepatitis you are, we hope, recovering from is not to be taken casually. Its potentially damaging effects on the liver are no light matter, and recurrence of it could be very serious. The possibility of venereal diseases, including herpes, is ever present in a promiscuous climate, and now especially there is "Morbus Kaposi," the exact nature of which is unknown but the deadly results of which are clear. This together with the mysterious weakening of the immune system which opens the gates to a variety of ills. The day after our talk on the phone I came across the enclosed article in *Der Spiegel*, the German news magazine. Its contents deserve your attention, even if you have to struggle with translation or find some translating help. Among other things, it suggests the likelihood that the use of marijuana and other drugs may be related to the problem of weakened immune systems.

So what is my point, or points? (1) That homosexuality and macho gay promiscuity are not necessarily synonymous, that the latter is highly unlikely to bring you fulfillment in either the short or the long run, and that the health risks it presents are so great that a wise person will certainly not run them; (2) that there is still a great deal about the impact of drug use—even light drug use—that is not understood (just what "responsible" drug use means is not clear); (3) that you should not allow yourself and your life to be so dominated by your gay sex life in all its dimensions that it wholly absorbs your energies and keeps you from being able to focus on other meaningful goals and desires you wish to pursue. Mind you, I'm not saying you are thus dominated, but several comments you made last week on the phone so strongly suggested a fatalistic acceptance of all the health hazards we were discussing that I wonder if you shouldn't strongly remind yourself of the *choices you can exercise. You* take charge of your life, don't let circumstances dictate your course.

You said you would run the risks, enjoy the ride, and if you were unlucky, bear the consequences. I've no doubt you would. That takes character, and I believe you have it. You said you'd kill yourself rather than linger as a burden to anyone. Well, that may or may not be an admirable resolve, but it may be considered admirable only if you do all possible to avoid arriving at that extremity. You cited the native cultures in which old or otherwise burdensome people voluntarily eliminate themselves. But I guarantee you that in those societies such people generally do everything they can first of all to be survivors.

Life is given us as a resource. I think we have a moral responsibility to husband it well. It ought not to be squandered, ought not to be rashly risked. I don't mean life should only be lived timidly, but I think one should live with the aim of being a survivor if one possibly can. Life has many rewarding facets and the possibility of some duration. So don't put all your chips on a few quick throws of the dice for just a limited return. You have a fine future ahead of you, Brad. I really believe that. Live partly for that future, and don't sacrifice too much for the present. That was Esau's mistake, you remember.

Should you resent the tone I've taken and feel I'm presumptuous to advise you, remember that any man, regardless of his age or experience, is fortunate to have caring friends of different persuasions who will share their views as touchstones.

Harry Truman once said, "The most important things one learns are learned *after* one already knows it all." I know I don't know it all, and I trust you'd acknowledge that you don't either. So let's keep flexible and continue to sift what comes our way.

———

25 July 1982

Dear Brad,

. . . We're all anticipating our California trip. Your mom hasn't had a real vacation in some time, Roger is eager to get some feel for things down there, especially in the Sacramento area, and of course Ted is more than ready to see additional parts of the world. I hope our coming to visit you is still compatible with your plans. Our intent is to leave home August 15 probably and reach L.A. about Friday, August 19. That way we can have the weekend with you.

Well, how are you feeling about the relocation to Hawaii by now? In one sense your disclosure came as a surprise; in another sense it is not surprising at all, at least not in the fact that you are discovering some good reasons to leave L. A. and your present environment. Exciting as the place is for you, and enticing as you find the fast-paced life there, you are—it seems—recognizing some negative dimensions to it, dimensions not compatible with your personal well-being immediately and in the long run. That your good judgment would bring you to this realization was something I expected to happen eventually, and that it apparently is occurring now is, I believe, all to the good. I have the impression that the gay life in L.A. is hedonistic to an extreme—and that brings with it not only the much publicized health dangers (which you would indeed be wise to take seriously) but also dangers to the psyche, the will, undermining your sense of purpose with a continuing and debilitating quest for sensations and nouveau experience. That way lie frustration and personal nihilism—which I am aware you do not want. I speak in general terms—and with no intent to preach.

I gather from your telephone remarks that your intended relocation is a result of two developments: (1) your recognition of these negative aspects of life in L.A. and a desire (with mixed feelings) to start in a somewhat different direction elsewhere, cultivating more consistently friends with positive attitudes and "simpler" lifestyles, avoiding the haunted dimensions of life in the ghetto; (2) your promising relationship with Drew, who apparently embodies these more positive values. And of course there is your general desire to see the world. Have I stated it correctly?

Well, the new start could certainly work to your personal advantage, Brad. That it would be fun to see Hawaii and live there for a time is obvious enough, but that is not the primary issue as I see it. Rather, the question is whether you will improve your situation in more vital respects. I do think that a stable, loving relationship will do much to give meaning to your life, if you can achieve it. It requires some renunciations, of course, but they are worth it for the sake of the positive benefits (see Ecclesiastes 4:8-12). You have had some experience now, and that should help you in sizing up Drew. Does he want the same things you do? What kind of renunciations is *he* willing to make for long-term happiness? And his health—could he pass a blood test, etc.? Will life with him help you to clarify and reach your career and personal goals—or otherwise?

As for the change in environment, Honolulu will doubtless also have a hedonistic gay community similar to that in L. A. if you seek it. The change in location will be positive only if it corresponds with a change in you and a resolve to redirect your life and habits. Certainly the right kind of friends will be a great help if this is what you want.

As for the financial aspects of it, you are in the best position to assess that. I expect your past experience will prevent you from getting burned again in the same ways. Just make sure your arrangements are cleanly made and clearly understood. I know you don't want any more holes to climb out of.

I guess these may sound like the words of a Polonius, a great piling up of platitudes. Well, make whatever use of them seems best to you. If you want to employ us as a further sounding board, we are always available.

I look forward to seeing you in a few weeks. I miss seeing you oftener. I confess the long distance between here and Hawaii saddens me some.

I pray for you always—after my fashion. Pray for us too— after yours.

Din Far

30 October 1982

Dear Brad,

. . . You remember last week that you made a few comments about work, especially about your feeling a bit disillusioned by the necessity of it. Then there followed a little exchange about the value of work *if* it is a means of connecting one to vital living rather than alienating one from life. A couple of days later I happened to be looking at a back issue of *Quest* and came upon an article entitled "Workers and Lovers." I've made an enclosed copy of it for you. I read it myself in the context of our telephone conversation, and I found several things in it that were thought provoking. It was interesting to me to make a little self-assessment in terms of the lists of conflicting values on page 16. I found myself to be partly worker, partly lover, the former especially by background and some of the values in my upbringing, the latter perhaps especially by virtue of my grounding in the humanities and sympathy with self-discovery and quality in one's living. I suppose, in other words, that my good fortune in finding a kind of work to do that is personally rewarding for the most part has helped me avoid becoming submerged in the worker mentality and has helped me avoid alienation in my work. Maybe you won't at all agree with my assessment of myself. Incidentally, I have no ulterior motive in sending the article. I'm sure you'll find much of it very compatible with your thinking. Perhaps you've seen it already.

Remember the xeroxed articles you sent home with me in August? I've read them with interest. The article on literary patronage—à la foundation and university support—was a new perspective on the subject for me, and useful, since that is a subject I sometimes talk about with students. Apropos of the articles on LSD, what can I say? To deny outright on the basis of my present personal experience (or lack of it) that the use of this drug can result in something positive for some people under the right conditions would be foolish. To deny that use of such a potent agent can be potentially dangerous, depending on the person and the conditions, also seems foolish to me. So I suppose you and others must make your personal choice, weigh the risks and the rewards. How does one intelligently weigh such a matter? Perhaps with reference to one's *whole* life and one's happiness in that whole perspective. Does use of such a drug alienate you from the reality to which you must inevitably return, or does it make that reality better, easier to sustain, happier? Does it make life in general a good experience, or does it leave one cloyed, disillusioned with the daily routine. I say this in relation to your remarks last week in which you expressed a degree of disillusionment about the future; you spoke of being jaded. I'm sorry to hear that, for at 24 the world and the future ought to be opening out, with a positive sense of desirable challenges and opportunities ahead. I don't want to jump to the conclusion that drug experience is necessarily responsible for your present feeling of alienation, but I do think that what I am suggesting here is a good way to assess any kind of experience at any stage of life: does it reconcile one to reality and make the possibilities within that reality seem richer.

Let me give you my considered testimony. On the whole, life is good, desirable. At times the world may seem mad (this has always been so, it is not just a reflection of present absurdity), but order and meaning on a small and personal scale are possible. *Happiness* may not be possible perpetually on a day-to-day basis, but *meaningful* living is—if there is something in one's life that one is willing to sacrifice for. This may be useful work that is rewarding, it may be goals of achievement that one is striving to reach, it may be someone who matters enough to work and sacrifice for. To be meaningful, life must be a challenge—otherwise it would get dull in a hurry. But to any intelligent, thoughtful individual, life's challenge cannot be other than apparent. It is not always easy to avoid alienation, cope with discouragement, and accept oneself. But with time, the focus sharpens, and meaning and satisfaction seem to be more consistently available. Your mom, for example, has struggled over the years for self-definition; and that struggle is now paying off. She is happier now, more confident, more accepting of herself, more capable, more creative, more relaxed, more fun to live with than ever. I too, though my pattern has been a different one, feel more relaxed, more self-accepting, find more pleasure in my environment, feel more in tune with my life.

Well, you can decide if there is anything of value in these beliefs of mine, this qualified optimism. Let me presume to offer a bit of advice: avoid whatever kind of experience leads to your feeling jaded, cultivate that which gives a sense of purpose, achievement, self-acceptance. You have a fine future to look forward to, and you have the equipment—mental and physical—to make the most of it.

Another onesided conversation, but we've had such good, intense talks that I can almost feel you are present here. Now I wait to hear your response—whenever a good and suitable occasion shall allow. You were right to remark on the phone that it would be so very nice to be together and have a long conversation. How would you like to come to snowy Idaho for Christmas?

With love, Dad

———

4 January 1983

Dear Brad,

At least a month has passed since that longish telephone conversation in which we talked of religion, and you said that your contact with the born-again Christian and his hyper-positive pronouncements had reawakened some old uncertainties in your mind. I trust that that mood has passed to some extent by now. Nevertheless, I know how someone like that can bowl one over temporarily, if, that is, one is of the type who acknowledges that some things in life seem uncertain, and what sane man doesn't? Then in blows the guy who *knows* all the answers, and all the answers are *simple!* It's the level of his confidence that causes one to pause and say, "Could this gullible fellow be right after all?" Well, I'll stake everything on his being wrong; otherwise God is demeaned and our human dignity and stature as his children are undermined.

Here are a few of the premises on which my religious faith rests:

1) God is not running us through an arbitrary obstacle course for his own glory and satisfaction; he is not interested in punishment as such. He is not a legalistic tyrant waiting to pounce when we stumble. These notions are contrary to the nature of a loving, patient God; they are contrary to the *dominant* tenor of Christ's teachings as we have them in the Gospels.

2) God wishes to foster our individual growth and development. He does not mean earth life to be primarily restrictive, inhibiting, but rather expansive and conducive to our progress.

3) In the long run, "rewards" and "punishments" are inherent in our deeds, our ways of living and being; they are not arbitrarily imposed from outside by a stern judge. Joseph Smith understood this, I think. In the Doctrine and Covenants occurs this passage which you will surely remember: "There is a law irrevocably decreed in heaven before the foundations of this world, upon which all blessings are predicated—And when we obtain any blessing from God, it is by obedience to that law upon which it is predicated" (130:20-21). I take this to mean that the consequences of our acts are inherent in the very nature of those acts. That is, doing good deeds for others generally makes us feel good and has a beneficial effect on the long range development of our character. Selfishness (i.e. preoccupation with self to a degree that an appropriate balance between the self and others is not maintained) does not lead to peace of mind or a good feeling about oneself. Being useful in the world, doing something that seems worthwhile with one's hours, brings satisfaction; idleness ultimately leaves one empty and dull and possibly frustrated. Etcetera. You can supply numerous examples as well as I. This is almost like saying that we create our own punishments and re-

wards—or choose them at least, but always within the eternal
law. And the law is eternal not because God said arbitrarily,
"Let it be so!" but rather because the relationship of acts and
their consequences are very consistent and have always been
so.

Such a view is consistent with my conviction that God is
interested in our growth, and that he allows us to work out our
paths in relation to what we learn through our ways of acting
and being. In this sense, "sin" is following courses that frustrate
our quest for growth, wholeness, harmony. "Sin" alienates us
from self and from others by creating barriers, stumbling blocks,
frustrations.

Clearly, then, we must assess the rightness or wrongness of our
behaviors by continually evaluating their results. Sometimes this is
easy because the results are obvious in the short run; other situations are more complex, and short term outcomes may not hold
consistently as time passes. But God is not keeping a book to effect
punishment. He simply allows us to become the sum of our acts.
That is his "judgment."

Because it is sometimes difficult to gauge the long term effects of
our acts, we can often assist ourselves by studying the lives of others,
the cumulative experience of the race. Still, that does not suffice by
itself. Existentially considering the truth of our own experience is
finally inescapable. That entails living with some uncertainties; that
means, as Sartre put it, that we are willing to assume the "burden
of freedom."

Apropos of your born-again friend and his assertions, you might
remember that Christ's statements in the Gospels are filled with a
number of striking ambiguities, paradoxes, even outright contradictions. The reborn Christians pick and choose rather restrictively,
but we must accept the gospel in its completeness and its complexity. Perhaps it's time for you to reread the Gospels yourself in order
to be able to point this out to him more effectively. More impor-

tantly, you may find a good deal of clarity for yourself by engaging those provocative texts from your present vantage point.

Enough for tonight. Love, Dad

Photos

Father and son, in Logan, spring 1959.

Brad with Roger, his next younger brother, in Logan, 1961.

Roger, Mom, and Brad sharing a bedtime story in Iowa City, 1965.

An early teenage "school picture" that captures the gentle side of his temperament.

Family portrait just prior to departure for sabbatical leave
in Denmark, November 1975. Clockwise: Brad, Roger, Sandra,
Ted, Mike, and Wayne.

Pocatello High School graduation, May 1977.

Family portrait, just before Brad left home to attend the University of Utah, 1978.

Living in Los Angeles, 1981.

Self-portrait in
dorm room at
Utah State
University,
1984.

With friend Donna during last visit to Los Angeles,
spring break, 1986.

On the front step at home in Pocatello, with best friend Scott,
Wayne, and Boots, September 1986.

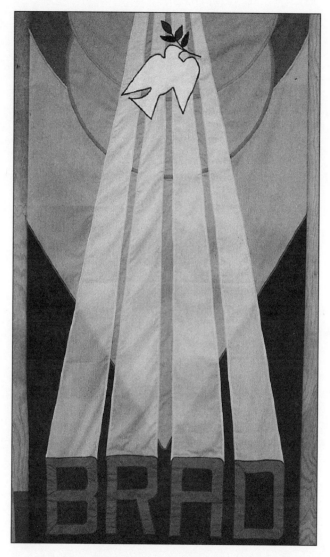

Sandra created this panel for the National AIDS Quilt.

IV. World Out of Joint
[August 1991]

As I look back on that period from June 1985, when Brad's illness became unmistakably apparent, to December 1986, when his life ended—as I consider the events that led up to it and followed from it, what stands out for me is the pervasive irony. It was a time when the smooth fabric of our lives was turned inside out, a time when the dependable vehicle in which we were riding unpredictably jumped the rails.

It was a time of contradictions, of incongruities. During that period we built a new house and moved into it, a process normally associated with optimism: but from the outset it was a dwelling in which our son was dying. The delight we felt on the occasion of Mike's wedding in August 1986 was undercut by the inexorable decline Brad was living out. When Ted left for a two-year prose-lyting mission in Uruguay a month later, our knowledge that his life was opening outward was companioned with our awareness of the closing down of Brad's.

It was a time when we donned masks and wore them every day. We never intended for it to be that way. We did not like the duplicity. But fate and society's ignorance and prejudice and our own pride and fear made actors of us. In front of the curtain we played our normal roles as well as we could, concealing our most urgent preoccupations. Sometimes we muffed our lines, sometimes we grew angry with our fellow actors. Behind the masks our turmoil seethed. We were bursting yet had to be contained.

Nothing from this period was more paradoxical than the experience of time. There were moments when day-to-day coping with small practical problems seemed like a sentence of perpetual tedium. On the other hand, we often felt as if on a roller coaster, careening through the weeks toward inevitable fatality with a momentum that was terrifying. At such times, this particular story had all too clearly not only a beginning and a middle but the prospect of a stark end. We discovered how near life is to death, yet how incredibly difficult it can be to reconcile them.

I want to describe here the existential disjuncture of this period. I want to write about that unending stream of illness- related practical problems with which we had to cope, about the practical implications of the philosophical and theological issues we were trying to untangle, about our struggle to salvage interpersonal relationships whose foundations were shaken. In a way these experiences were all so miscellaneous that I'm afraid the examples I cite may seem a hodgepodge. But keep in mind that that is partly the point.

Though the plot complication of our family story from this period blindsided us, not all the ironies that followed from it were bad. When it became apparent on Brad's return from college that he was not well enough to take up his tools as a family carpenter in the construction of our new house, he scheduled an appointment with an internal medicine specialist. Was his student health insurance in force over the summer? I asked him. Summer coverage was optional for a small additional premium, he said, but he had neglected to extend it. Was it now too late to do so? He telephoned that same afternoon, a Thursday, to find out: the deadline for summer coverage was the following day. Next morning he drove one hundred miles from Pocatello to Logan to sign the request form and pay the premium.

That student health insurance covered the cost of the appendectomy he underwent two weeks later. It covered a subsequent hospital stay to overcome a serious postoperative infection. It covered the ongoing consultations and tests over the summer. Even more crucially, that renewal of student health insurance, so narrowly accomplished, carried with it a conversion privilege that enabled him in September, no longer a student, to secure as an individual subscriber a health insurance policy with Blue Shield of Idaho. While the new monthly premium was substantial, it amounted over the next fifteen months to only a small fraction of the sum Blue Shield paid toward defraying subsequent treatment costs. Without the conversion privilege, and with knowledge of his pre-existent condition, Blue Shield would have rejected his policy application.

The blood analyses done early that summer disclosed worrisome irregularities, indications congruent with several dire diagnoses, including AIDS and leukemia. That kind of news gets one's attention. But I have always felt that the worst scenario is usually not the most likely to occur, and so initially I persuaded myself that a less serious explanation would eventually surface. In fact, the confirmation of the presence of HIV antibodies was not long in coming.

But antibodies do not mean necessarily that one will develop AIDS. Even if the patient exhibited preliminary symptoms such as fever, night sweats, appetite loss, weight loss, nausea, and cough, which in combination were in 1985 called the ARC syndrome (a precondition of AIDS), it was believed based on evidence available then that ARC would lead to full-blown AIDS in only about 35 percent of cases. In the years of which we are speaking, a formal and official confirmation of AIDS required diagnosis of either pneumocystis pneumonia or Kaposi sarcoma, opportunistic diseases characteristically associated with acquired immune deficiency. After 1987 the official AIDS definition was expanded to allow confirmation by the presence of several additional opportunistic diseases.

As the summer progressed, Brad experienced increasingly the symptoms of ARC. Yet we did not have a confirmed diagnosis of

AIDS, and I kept my mind fixed on that percentage of cases in which ARC would apparently not reach AIDS. Gene Ratcliff, Brad's physician, kindly did not disabuse me of my hope based on technical and somewhat arbitrary definition. But he did refer Brad to a communicable disease specialist in another city for evaluation. She did not mince words. "He has AIDS," she said to Sandra in a curt voice devoid of any apparent sympathy. She was standing several yards away in the next room. "Most likely it will be a slow death. Come back when he has difficulty swallowing, or when diarrhea is unmanageable." I dismissed this grim prognosis by simply blocking it out. How could she possibly know for sure so "prematurely"? What did she know about our faith and Brad's will?

Meanwhile we had to deal with the PR and FR (family relations) demands of our situation. We hardly knew what to tell people. That Brad was homosexual was known within the extended family by only three pairs of aunts and uncles. Among our general acquaintances, and among Brad's childhood and teenage friends in this community, none had been told by him or by us. How were we now to explain this substantial illness he had developed?

As it turned out, with a good deal of hedging and vagueness: "Well, he has apparently some kind of virus which saps his strength. It has left him exhausted, somewhat in the way of mononucleosis. The physicians are still trying to pin it down, but there's nothing conclusive yet. Could be quite a number of things." Etcetera. Not quite a literal lie, strictly speaking (there was still no *confirmed diagnosis* according to official definition), but pretty evasive. We did not mention the overwhelming likelihood of AIDS. I remember in early August attending an extended family reunion, and after hearing our explanation my cousin's husband, a chemistry professor, said: "It sounds a lot like AIDS." "Oh good heavens," Sandra replied, "I certainly hope not."

It was a shameful deception, in more ways than one. Looking back, I find it incredible that we maintained this facade with our acquaintances (excepting only a few persons) for as long as we did. In particular, I find it ironic in the extreme that within an extended

family I had always considered loving and close-knit we could not
express our anxiety. Whom were we trying to protect, and from
what? Was it Brad, who, we thought, would suffer in the opinion
of some of them when they discovered he was gay? Was it our
parents, Brad's grandparents, who we thought would be caused
extraordinary pain by that revelation? Or was it ourselves, because
we were still not able to accept the stigma of homosexuality in our
immediate family? Were we all somehow afraid to acknowledge that
we as an extended family were not perfect according to a prescribed
pattern, or even more alarming, that the pattern itself might be out
of touch with reality and therefore flawed. As I view it now, this
behavior on our part reveals the presence of dysfunctionality where
I would like to have denied it. Somehow the religious attitudes
powerfully established in our greater family made us false to one
another.

Brad's condition worsened through the fall. In late October
life-threatening pneumocystis pneumonia set in. There followed
ten days in the intensive care unit and concurrent announcement
in the local newspaper of southeast Idaho's first confirmed case of
AIDS (the patient's anonymity was preserved). In the face of these
developments we could no longer avoid disclosing to additional
members of our greater family the nature of Brad's illness. Particularly those who were likely to visit our home. We thought they
should be able to decide if they wanted to see Brad before he died
and if they wished to risk exposure to the disease—to eat at our
table, to use our bathrooms. Some of them, as it turned out, didn't.

But with other acquaintances, we stayed closeted. Besides inertia, there were compelling reasons to do so. Nineteen-eighty-six
stands out as the year the general public finally got the message that
AIDS was real and a threat to the whole population. You could not
pick up a newspaper or magazine or turn on the television without
hearing about this frightening disease and those who transmitted
it. No longer was this a phenomenon confined to San Francisco and
New York. Everyone in the provinces was now being explicitly
warned. Misinformation about its transmission was widely re-

peated. Suddenly fear was rampant, a lot of anger and intolerance expressed, even violence was perpetrated against some AIDS sufferers and their families. With rhetorical excess, prominent politicians advocated identifying publicly those diagnosed with AIDS, isolating them on islands, branding homosexuals. One did not have to be paranoiac to recognize how much bigotry was out there, and how explicitly it was expressed, even in Pocatello.

Whatever inclination we may have felt to acknowledge openly our son's illness and his gay identity ran up against that awareness. And so we kept ourselves in isolation partly imposed, partly self-chosen. We seldom invited people to our home—an awkward and uncharacteristic stance, especially at a time when our friends and acquaintances were curious about our new dwelling. ("We'd like to come and see your new house." "Sure, that would be nice. We'll give you a call—sometime soon.")

In addition to this ongoing necessity of responding to well-intended inquiries (what do you say, for example, in the drugstore when casual acquaintances ask what brings you to the prescription counter?), we faced other pressures. Not least among them were all the decisions and uncertainties and frustrations that come in dealing with the health care establishment when a loved one is seriously ill.

How do you choose a personal physician, the one who is most knowledgeable about your disease and how to treat it, one who will be supportive, tolerant, accessible? If you have an exotic new killer disease that few physicians in southeast Idaho have even seen, does it make sense to remain here for treatment when in Los Angeles there are doctors who have been treating AIDS patients by the score for half a decade? More than a few of Brad's friends in L.A. urged him to return to southern California. He weighed the alternatives. We in our supporting role pondered the matter.

Inevitably, in deciding among health care alternatives, one must consider financial implications and support resources. Where would he live if he went back to L.A.? Who would care for him when he required constant assistance? Unable to work, without a job and an income, how could he meet living expenses? While these difficulties were not insurmountable, they were nevertheless formidable. On the other hand, if he stayed in Idaho he had a haven and ready support from us, though coming home and living under the parental roof when you have been independent for six years is not particularly what a young man desires. As for medical care, Brad reasoned that doctors in L.A. had no miraculous cures, that a competent practitioner in Pocatello could probably do as well for him. Moreover, he had quickly come to respect Gene Ratcliff, with whom he developed a fine rapport. Having decided to put his case in Dr. Ratcliff's hands, I do not think he ever entertained doubts about it.

Nor, after our initial uncertainty, did I. Ratcliff proved a tremendous support for him—and for us. He respected, cared about, and became emotionally involved in Brad's case. With local hospital administrators and staff, state health officials, news media personnel, and others, Ratcliff was a fierce champion of his patient's rights and interests.

During that year and a half numerous others in our local health care community responded in their various capacities with similar professional competence and compassion—some hospital and home care nurses, for example, physical therapists, hospice workers, lab personnel. Remember that in 1985 and 1986 this could not be taken for granted. In the provinces few health care workers knew much about AIDS beyond its killer reputation, and many felt very much at risk in dealing with someone afflicted by it.

Brad's hospitalization in November 1985 underscored this point. He had firmly resisted this step, but with the onset of pneumonia his condition deteriorated so rapidly and dramatically, culminating in a fever-induced convulsion, that we had to summon an ambulance. To our surprise and irritation, what arrived at our curb in response was not merely an ambulance but also a large fire truck, lights flashing, siren wailing, with a resuscitator and four attendants. They charged in with good intentions, insisted on completing a time-consuming protocol of questioning that seemed less than fully needed, managed to knock over a humidifier full of water, and generally created mini havoc. When they discovered that the person they were conveying in all likelihood had AIDS, they were angry and almost refused to complete their task. They arrived at the emergency room full of complaint, and only warnings from Ratcliff silenced them.

After a lung biopsy confirmed pneumocystis and, now officially, AIDS, Brad was taken to the intensive care unit. The next day, when his blood oxygen level fell to a point incompatible with life, he was attached to the respirator. In the ICU stringent protocols were established for nurses and visitors. Initially, all of us had to wear masks, gowns, gloves. We had to wash our hands on entering and leaving. Some of the nurses, obviously reluctant and terrified by exposure to the carrier of this plague, covered themselves most meticulously. (Two or three even declined to work in this danger-ous situation.) The attending physicians, who knew more about transmission of AIDS, did not bother to put on this protective armor, nor did some of the more confident nurses and technicians.

The extreme sanitary measures were doubtless well intended, and I understand that they function to protect the patient. Never-theless, the protection was symbolically apt: it bespoke, and under-scored for emphasis, the "unclean" status of this patient, an unclean-ness that for some of the nurses included the abhorrent and "untouchable" condition of homosexuality. If the patient feels feared or in some way despised by those who provide his care, and Brad rightly recognized such attitudes in several of his nurses, that state of mind is hardly conducive to comfort and healing.

I remember vividly my gratitude to those nurses whose natural manner and conversation consistently rose to the challenge of this special case. One ICU nurse in particular caught Brad's imagination. This fellow was an avid falconer in his spare time. He described vividly to Brad the care and training of the raptors. "When you're feeling better," he said matter-of-factly, "why don't you drive up and spend some time with me and my guys out in the field. And you can watch them tear apart the chicks I raise to feed them." This as if Brad's recovery were a foregone conclusion. Though precariously ill and silenced by a breathing tube in his throat, he seized eagerly on the prospect of this outing.

One year later when Brad was hospitalized during the final week of his life, the nursing staff had grown in experience, knew more about AIDS and how to deal with it safely and confidently. I remember one nurse especially whose compassionate, accepting manner eased that ordeal for all of us. One morning a couple of days before the end, she was, with gloved hand, helping him to overcome the effects of severe constipation. "Now bear down," she said; "I can feel it coming, that's good; we've got to get it out, keep pushing." Brad, lying on his stomach and only semi-clear headed, opened his eyes and fixed them on his mother seated at the bedside: "*What* is going on here?" he said incredulously. "Am I having a baby, *or what?*"

Even under the best of conditions, with the greatest good will on everyone's part, the delivery of health care can be laced with stress and frustration. When a loved one is suffering, delay seems intolerable, inaccessibility is maddening. Waiting for a return call from a busy physician leaves one feeling so powerless, so off stride. One paces back and forth, physically, mentally. And when someone is assigned to cover for an absent regular doctor, one doubts that the substitute "fully" understands the situation with all of its contextual nuances. After all, the choice of a *personal* physician involves a *personal* relationship, built on familiarity and trust. When that reassuring element is missing, even impeccable treatment by a substitute seems to fall short. Then there are the times when the problem is not the physician's inaccessibility but rather the question of whether, given ambiguities in the condition of the patient and given one's own exaggerated anxieties, one ought to bother the busy doctor at all. I remember more than a few occasions when I fretted over whether a call was justified.

The world and its institutions are imperfect, and in the throes of illness one resents that. I remember one summer evening taking Brad to the hospital emergency room. He was nauseated and feverish. We were ushered into a brightly-lit examination area to wait. The room was excessively air-conditioned. I was cold, Brad was shaking. I could not find anyone who was able (or willing) to alter the room temperature, and it was a long time before I could get anyone to supply him with a blanket. We waited—and waited—and waited—before he was finally seen by a brusque on-call physician, who, I thought, discussed Brad's symptoms as if he were dealing with a crop report. Stonefaced, he showed not the slightest recognition of the human dimension.

We lapsed into Kafkaesque absurdities in other areas. Anyone who has had to consult numerous specialists, visit care centers for tests and treatments, purchase prescriptions and other medical supplies, knows what it means to be buried under billings and insurance forms. Nothing seems to be standardized: the neurologist's forms are unlike the opthalmologist's; the surgeon requires that you file your own insurance claims; the insurance company's communications value convenience more than clarity; every office or agency has different systems, different policies. When one is ill or stressed and taxed for time, such idiosyncracies afford little amusement.

One thinks of Kafka's protagonist K. who, having reached the outer precincts of the inscrutable Castle, encounters with amazement a seemingly endless array of files and official paperwork. He senses that they may relate importantly to his case, but he has no clue how to access them. Like Kafka, I found in this confusing and irritating battery of business documents a bizarre symbol of disjunction—the impersonal face of the health care establishment, seemingly impervious to the existential anxiety that derives from human illness.

The pressure of dealing with the outside world became increasingly compounded by intrafamily stresses. It is natural that tensions arise in families due to differences of temperaments, priorities, generational and gender perspectives. Under the best of conditions, these are accommodated and minimized. But when there are too many demands, too few resources to meet them, and too little outlet for emotion, normally good relationships become brittle. I state the obvious. Over the years our family has done, I suppose, as well as most in managing our differences, but before Brad's ordeal was over we all felt the lacerations of blame and frustration.

Toward the end Brad's temper was uneven. Mostly he was gentle and patient. But as his sense of autonomy declined, as he grew increasingly dependent even in small matters, his frustration could erupt in sarcasm or anger. Those who stood by, who loved him and tried to ease his pain, were on those occasions the innocents on whom his wrath fell. He would apologize—but the hurt lingered.

One facet of this internal tension was sharply focused in late October 1985 as Brad slipped into the throes of what proved to be pneumocystis pneumonia. It can be difficult for laypeople to assess just how ill a person is and how much immediate professional attention is needed. Brad emphatically did not want to be hospitalized, and he protested that his symptoms could be treated at home. Ambivalently, I accepted his assessment of the situation. Sandra, more sensitive to his real condition than I, pressed hard to give Ratcliff power to hospitalize him. We had a standoff for forty-eight hours during which time she remained in his room to minister to his needs. She knew his condition was sinking rapidly, and she was frustrated with our denial and male stoicism. For her, it was a confrontation of masculine and feminine ways of understanding and evaluating. Following this incident, she felt increasingly isolated and powerless in an otherwise all-male household whenever her feelings ran counter to Brad's and to my wait-and-see, tough-it-out mentality.

Aside from Brad, it was Sandra who bore the brunt of the long ordeal. Gene Ratcliff observed that it was she who steadied us all and kept us from unraveling. He admired her for her grit and was surprised that she had held together so well. She had done so at considerable cost. She had been the essential care giver, day in, day out. She had done most of the nursing, had been the manager who dealt with all the daily details. She was the first line of advice and support, the listening ear when Brad (or any of the rest of us) needed to talk, or the closest target when he needed to vent his anger. It was she who was always half awake at night, listening for him much as she had done twenty-seven years earlier, she who could sense when he needed assurance to get him through the night. Mostly it was a twenty-four-hour-a-day job, and she filled it for eighteen months.

"What kind of support system did you have?" people have since asked her. The fact is, almost no one knew what she was enduring. Of the few family members and friends in whom she had confided, most were not nearby or were seriously troubled by the socio-re-ligious-health aspects of the situation as they perceived them. There were no organized groups in the community at that time to assist people confronting homosexuality or AIDS. Even I was not there sufficiently to share her load.

Incredibly, I was still trying to carry on business as usual, taking care of most of my faculty responsibilities, not telling anyone in the department about things at home, keeping up minimally with church duties. And I continued to do this until almost the end of Brad's life. Some of us are creatures of our training to such an extent that we do not even ask if there is any virtue in continuing to pull in harness. Not that I was detached from what was happening at home. But why didn't I see at the time that I could give myself permission to miss some working hours and to let others assume my church tasks?

Perhaps that was my way of coping. Clinging to the reassuring familiarity of the daily round was my informal support system, a feeble attempt to hold absurdity at bay. But near the end this subconscious strategy was not enough. I remember during the last week of Brad's life being so full of grief that I broke my closeted silence. "My son is in the hospital; he is dying," I told one of my longtime colleagues. I fought back tears. He was so surprised, and so full of compassion for me. It had not occurred to us that our friends would understand and stand by us.

After Mike's marriage in August, he left with his bride to live in Boise, and we saw them infrequently. Ted departed for Uruguay in early September. About the middle of October, Roger resigned his position as office manager of a small manufacturing firm in Santa Barbara and came home to be with the three of us. His intent was partly to buoy up Mom and Dad, partly to take his leave of Brad, his brother closest in age and boyhood experience. For him this was a family thing, and he wanted to be involved.

When we moved to 20th Street in late May, Brad occupied a bedroom on the second floor. He felt no enthusiasm for the new house, partly because he preferred places with some history or antiquity, even more perhaps because in the final months of his life he wanted to be surrounded by a familiar environment. We did not yet have a landscaped yard, and there were still unfinished interior details about the house. I believe he felt, after we moved, as if he were camping.

This uprootedness was not lessened when in late July his aching legs could no longer negotiate stairs without difficulty. His second floor bedroom was problematic, but the main floor possibilities were limited. There was only a sun room connected by French doors to the dining room. The former was not large, but it was light, and it had the further virtue of being sufficiently close to the living area so that Brad could occupy it without being cut off from the life of the household. So we set about organizing it as a bedroom, fitting its numerous windows with louvered blinds, installing an air conditioner. The brick-faced tromb wall, with its thermal mass, provided effective sound insulation from household noise.

In an effort to make his days pleasurable, we set up a TV in his room, brought in some books by Mann, Marquez, and Faulkner, and subscribed to *The New Yorker, The Nation, Vanity Fair,* and *Atlantic.* But he found little satisfaction in reading during those last few months. He could not focus or sustain his attention: I do not know if that was because his illness wearied him and drained his concentration, or if as the sand of his life ran out the ideas and issues of those books and periodicals simply lacked relevance. As for television, which as an adult he had not watched much anyway, I thought he might find some programs to pass his time. It engaged him almost not at all. "I can't stand watching one more nature program," he said in summary.

A year earlier I had urged him to write about what was happening to him. I knew that he had raw talent, that he was a keen ironist as well as a good observer. I thought writing might be something for him to look forward to each day and that, if it engaged him intensely, it might offer some detachment. But the compulsion was not in him. It came as a somewhat disillusioning revelation that this young man with such strong literary and aesthetic interests found so little consolation in them at the last.

But there was one activity that, surprisingly, did occupy him in the final months. He purchased a short wave radio, and during the long nights when he could not sleep he listened to a variety of overseas broadcasts. In the morning he was pleased to tell me of the far-flung places and issues he had encountered. I have not fully grasped why this interested him so.

Eventually we all came to the point of acknowledging that time was short, that what remained was at most a matter of several weeks. We were kept sane by the intensified demands of nursing: food, water, medication, clothing and bedding changes, bathing, massage, conversation about practical matters, consultations with physicians and other healthcare people. As long as there are demands, one responds.

But this was inevitably the culmination of the year-long summing up process. A letter Brad wrote in November to Joyce Parsons, a friend from his school years, captures the mood. Living in Arizona, Joyce heard from friends that Brad was ill, and she wrote to him a note of concern, delicately avoiding direct mention of AIDS.

"Dear Joyce," he responded,

> Your card was, as you said, a surprise but a very nice one, near enough to my birthday to be like an unexpected present.
>
> It's funny that you should have written just now. I have talked with my mother many times recently about you and about how much the childhood years spent on South 9th with you (especially),

also the friendship from high school and college, have meant to me. I have been completing a scrapbook and had cut out that wonderful picture of you at the Poky tricycle races from the old yearbook. It was a favorite of mine and deserves a place in my book. And too, I would like you and James to know that I think of your reception often. Your wedding and garden party afterward were delightful, exactly what I would have wanted had I married.

Unfortunately, this is now closed to me. I was diagnosed with AIDS in July of last year, the result of my profligate life in Los Angeles. Most likely I have been carrying the virus several years since my departure, but it came as no real surprise. In November '85 I was admitted to the hospital with pneumocystis pneumonia (common in AIDS patients). Ten days in intensive care, subsequent recovery, a short remission of the disease, and then rapid decline. I have been living at home with my parents since my diagnosis. Things at this point are quite difficult. Although I have been lucky to have suffered less than some patients and have experienced tremendous, almost incredible, support from my family and friends, quality in my life at this point is basically nonexistent. My body endures, it seems, only to suffer, and I am at a loss to understand the usefulness of this. I hope and pray to die soon, and although I feel some ambivalence about this, I do not feel afraid but look forward to death's tranquil peace.

I hope my telling you about this does not seem inappropriate. I tell you because I have spent much time during the past year in reflection on my life, and I find that I am delighted to have known you. You played an important part in my story, and somehow I feel that connection is not going to be broken.

As I said, it was wonderful to hear from you. I hope you and James are happy and content. So it sounds. I think of you often with affection.

Love, Brad

Several weeks later when Brad's ordeal ended, we were left to deal with the aftermath and to try to regain our equilibrium. I remember so vividly, now after five years, my feelings relative to his passing: death seemed so awesome, so outrageous, so terribly final, yet under the circumstances so welcome. Like Brad, we were ready to regard it as a blessed release for him, and no doubt for us as well. Though you would like to think your feelings are entirely selfless and focused on your loved one, in the last days when death is inevitable you anticipate the lifting of the burden. But you do not think of that when your son is lying there in the final throes of dying. I remember yet how, on returning home from the hospital that night after one o'clock, it was like coming numbly into a vast emptiness.

Following death, practical arrangements must be made, details attended to. It is not a time when one feels like seeing to them. There is (usually) a public ritual that must be gotten through, a communal process that sums up a life and allows those who remain to express their grief formally. We had pressing decisions to make relative to this process, but they did not lead to the post-mortem rituals characteristically practiced in our religious community.

When we spoke of these arrangements with Brad late in his life, he was adamant that he wanted neither a public announcement of his death nor a funeral service. That seemed sad to me, almost a denial of his existence. Perhaps he saw it also in that light and preferred it for that reason. He was still not willing to announce in his home town, even indirectly, that he was homosexual, that his life had finally come to this. At least that was the inference I drew. And when I remonstrated that we were proud of him, that we wanted his life acknowledged, and urged him to give his consent, he would not relent. "Maybe you could just have a happy wake here at home with a few friends," he allowed finally. I am absolutely certain he did not want to have a Mormon funeral, at which in the end the last word would be pronounced by someone who would find his identity unacceptable.

Our dilemma was compounded by the fact that we had been so close-mouthed about his illness. How could we now respect Brad's express requests and still communicate these developments to others in a suitable way? Though it was not an ideal solution, we decided to send a letter to relatives and friends. In all, we sent out roughly two hundred fifty letters, as follows:

Dear Friends,

We are writing this to let you know that Brad, our eldest son, passed away on Friday, December 5. Prior to his death he asked that there be no public announcement of the fact and that there be no funeral; we intend to honor these requests. But since you are among those who care for him and for us, we want you to know something of the circumstances of a life which ended prematurely.

There were several physical conditions that contributed to Brad's demise, all of which are traceable to an undermined immune system. He had AIDS, a fact of which he and we became aware in the summer of 1985. He had returned that June from his studies at Utah State University to assist us in the construction of a new home. As it turned out, he was not able to join in our family carpentry, but during the next year and a half, while he was living with us, he shared with us a far more significant experience, one that expanded our awareness and changed our lives.

Following an appendectomy in that first month, his condition worsened through the summer and fall. In October pneumocystis pneumonia crept on him, confirming definitively the AIDS diagnosis. Early in November he spent two weeks in the intensive care unit, where he very nearly died. But outstanding medical care and the support and prayers of friends and loved ones, together with his own renewed will to live, helped him to survive. There was then a period of remission during which he gained weight and strength and made plans for the future. He took a course at ISU during spring semester, though often he was, in fact, feeling too miserable for it; still determined, he took another course during the early summer and finished it sheerly on will power. Meanwhile, the remission had ended in April, and his suffering recommenced and steadily intensified. AIDS is indeed a formidable antagonist; he fought it to the best of his ability, courageously. In the process he learned—and we learned vicariously—what it means to have a vigorous healthy body dismantled, ounce by ounce, nerve by nerve.

You could not call him lucky, but he was at least more fortunate than some AIDS victims. He did not develop Kaposi Sarcoma, the skin cancer that often occurs with AIDS; though he lost the sight in one eye toward the end and experienced occasional limited paralysis and, of course, dramatic loss of weight and strength, his mind remained alert and clear virtually to the end.

The extra year granted him after his near death in November 1985 was a beneficial gift to him as well as to us. He did not fully understand the necessity of the added suffering he experienced, nor do we, but he profited from the time to sort out and evaluate much in his personal philosophy. We will not forget the conversations we had as the days and nights passed. That year encompassed a time of profound emotional and spiritual significance for all of us.

Brad's last week was spent in the hospital after it became impossible for us to provide for his medical needs and his comfort at home. The end was not easy, but there were some periods of tranquility for him during the last several days. We were with him when he died. He had wished to be cremated, and so we helped to prepare him and to dress him in the clothing he had chosen. At that point we stood as a family around his hospital bed and thanked God for the gift of Brad's life among us.

We are very proud of our son and of the courage and integrity with which he faced the difficult circumstances of his life. In this we refer not only to his terminal illness but also to the fact of his homosexuality, of which we have known for some eight years. Our experience during that time has taught us that society generally and organized religions in particular have much to answer for in their treatment of homosexual men and women. We earnestly pray that our own church as well as others will come to regard these people with greater tolerance, accepting in the spirit of Christian love those whom God has so created.

We said at the outset that Brad died prematurely; that is true only in a narrow sense. In the larger perspective, we perceive a completeness within the span of his twenty-eight years. He managed to live intensely, to burn brightly while he was among us. We feel his experience will be immensely beneficial for those who have known him and for others who will come to know indirectly what he stood for. But mostly we believe his experience will be valuable to him as he now goes on to continue his eternal progression. At the time of his death, as we contemplated the features of a face sharpened by starvation, his mother said, "He looks like an eagle, and now he is soaring beautifully."

We will miss him greatly.

If the weeks ahead afford an opportunity, we will be glad to speak with you about Brad and our experience with him.

Sincerely,

Sandra and Wayne Schow

Some of those who got this letter shared it with others. In an irregular fashion, the word got around. And then, quite suddenly, we were free to talk about it all—mostly. After virtually hiding Brad's illness for eighteen months, his homosexuality for nearly eight years, we had them out in the open. It was as liberating as if a great blockage were removed and real honesty were finally possible. How strange but how good that felt. What a pity that it took us so long.

I say "mostly" free to talk about it. At least there were now no practical dangers to Brad in the revelation. And the ice was surely broken in terms of the knowledge becoming public. The only remaining barriers to openness with others were those vestiges of fear, shame, or inertia within ourselves which sometimes were unpredictably manifested. One ironic example remains fixed in my mind. About three weeks after Brad's death, Roger encountered at the mall just after Christmas two sisters whom he and Brad had known well in high school. He had not seen them for several years. After some conversation, one of them asked: "How's Brad?" Clearly, she knew nothing of his illness.

"He's fine."

"Is he home for Christmas?"

"Yes," Roger replied, "this Christmas he's home." End of topic.

"And you left it at that!" exclaimed his mother incredulously when Roger told us that evening about the encounter. "Why didn't you say what's happened, why didn't you explain yourself?"

"I don't exactly know," he said. "On one level my answers were true, and I didn't feel like going into it just then."

The next day he called Margaret and cleared up the dramatic irony in their previous conversation, doubtless with ambivalent feelings. Vestiges. We all showed them at times. I think they lingered somewhat longer in our sons than for Sandra and me, but for them too it grew easier in time to speak with others of Brad's death and its causes.

How ironic it is that AIDS, which in the United States has found its most frequent target in gay men, has done more to advance understanding of homosexuality than virtually any other influence. Not because AIDS directly explains homosexuality—its causes or its particular ethos—but simply because for the general public in the United States AIDS made confrontation with homosexuality unavoidable. By several means, the virus has become the most powerful closet door opener in modern history.

On one level, it made the public aware that homosexual people are to be found all around us, often where we least expect them to be, that they include people whose lives and achievements we have admired. Highly publicized cases have certainly had an impact. But for most of us AIDS illustrates these realizations nearer to home. Today there are but few who do not know someone—a family member, a friend, or a colleague—who is HIV positive, has AIDS, or has succumbed as a result of it. And where this occurs, it most often comes with a revelation of homosexual activity as the cause.

Public dialogue about homosexuality is commonplace today. What is said in the media and elsewhere would have been unthinkable a decade ago. People talk about real gay men and lesbians rather than stereotypes, reevaluating the premises on which their intolerance was based. Most knowledgeable men and women now recognize that there is not just one homosexual lifestyle but a variety of lifestyles—like the variety found among heterosexuals. Public exposure has brought home the realization that homosexual lives, like heterosexual lives, ought to be judged on their merits, and that gay and lesbian lives can be richly rewarding, beneficial to society as well as to individuals.

Paradoxically, the world that was for us not long ago so far out of joint begins now to show some evidence of better alignment as a result of what has happened. I wish we had not lost Brad. It seems so pointless and unjust. But there is some satisfaction in knowing that his shortened life contributed to this adjustment of cultural consciousness, this opportunity to reassess our attitudes and values. His case is not one of the famous examples, to be sure, but among them all he is the person who influenced one particular circle of family members and friends. Through them the rings of that influence continue to emanate outward as when a stone is thrown into water.

V. Grieving
[Fall 1989]

"I have been one acquainted with the night," says Robert Frost in a well-known poem. I can edit that line a little and say, "I have become one acquainted with grief." The verb "acquainted" is precisely accurate with its suggestion of direct and unmediated experience.

I did not realize how much I would miss Brad. Now, three years after his death, not a day passes without his being in my thoughts. There is so much to remind me of him. He lived with a surprising range of interests and enthusiasms: history, politics, urban culture, certain kinds of western landscape, literature, family relationships, philosophy, theology, weather, psychology, music and visual art, the impact of style in all facets of culture. His sticky mind contained a wealth of eclectic information.

To be around Brad was unavoidably to have one's awareness expanded. I was continually arrested by his views, by his taste, by his way of experiencing the world. His aesthetic sensibilities were strong, his crap detector well-developed. Continually he provoked and challenged my conventional wisdom. That was not always comfortable, but it was unquestionably valuable to me. He was so intense. What he liked he cared for passionately; what he didn't he abhorred. His moods were similarly up or down. He was not always measuredly rational, and he was not always easy to live with, but he heightened the impact of anything around you he regarded. Any time you spent with him was memorable.

Because so little around him escaped his notice or comment, because his interests corresponded at so many points with my own, my daily experiences in all of these areas continuously reinvoke him.

Certain places are especially potent to release the flood of memory, places like our old neighborhood on South Ninth where Brad and his brother Roger and their friends roamed the yards and alleys, played kid games, got into kid mischief, and learned a good bit about the world; places like our spot of ground on the semi-rural hills of Johnny Creek, south of town, where Brad grew to love the views over the narrow valley and the Portneuf Gap beyond, the sunsets startling the deeply furrowed northeastern hills into sharp relief, dramatic summer thunderstorms, and the solitude of the wooded ravine dropping below our house. It was an environment made to order for a romantic teenaged boy.

During the last year or so of Brad's life, we frequented a spot up on one of the benches on the east side of the city, which commanded a panoramic view. You can see the mountains cradling Pocatello and the Portneuf Valley to the south, with snow-capped Scout Mountain in the center of this fine vista. This was a spot important to both of us, not only for its austere beauty, which was never quite the same from one day to another, but for the fact that we two walked and talked there, or, as it became increasingly difficult for him to walk, simply sat and discussed what was important to us at the time. Because Brad associated himself so powerfully with these places, I cannot visit any of them without waves of nostalgia pouring over me.

There are those who, with good intentions, attempt to help those of us who grieve by removing from our lives reminders of what is gone. That is not what we want. These memories—these crumbs of a Madeleine—are not something we wish to be done with. We want to remember.

One of the things I have learned about sorrow is that often we grieve most keenly for the loss of what we really never had but only anticipated. We are sustained in life so greatly by our hopes for the future, by projected scenarios involving ourselves and our loved ones, and when these fail to be realized we feel we have been deprived of what seems already rightfully ours.

When Brad told us in 1979 that he was gay, I denied the validity of his assertion. For a variety of reasons, it was unthinkable. But as weeks passed, and as his truth was borne home to us, both Sandra and I experienced a long period of intense, multifaceted grief. Much of that was our mourning the obliteration of some of our fondest hopes for his future—and ours. We mourned the loss of anticipated family relationships that would have been simpler, easier, safer for all of us because they would have been based on conventional unities. We mourned the loss of what would have been a less perplexing life for Brad because he would not have had so much to fight against the current. We mourned the loss of our daughter-in-law, the wife he would never have. We did not even consider that a male companion would bring compensating satisfaction. Especially, we grieved for the grandchildren, Brad's children, who would never come. It seemed hard that he, who had understood the magic of childhood so well and always responded so warmly to little people around him, would never realize the challenges and joys of parenthood.

Our projected scenario was not to be. It had never really been promised. With time we came to accept by degrees Brad's orientation and to realize that it brought other possibilities for fulfillment. Yet I think I have even now not entirely put aside—and perhaps never will—the gut feeling that some things that were rightfully mine were stolen.

Once earlier in my life I experienced the untimely death of a loved one. In 1966 my youngest brother Paul was killed in a one-car accident. He skidded in the rain on oil-slick asphalt paving and plunged over an embankment. He was not quite sixteen. In perfect health, with all of the rich promise of his life before him, he was suddenly no longer in our midst.

As a youth and as a young adult, I had seen my grandfathers and then my grandmothers pass away. I cared for them, and would miss them, but they had fulfilled their years. The young especially do not grieve for long when death comes in timely fashion and releases the old from their burdens. But premature death is something else. When a loved one is erased even as he stands on the threshold of maturity, the event lacks the naturalness that could reconcile us to it.

We came from Iowa to Idaho for Paul's funeral. We mourned with our loved ones. We viewed the scene of the accident, we heard the explanations. We tried to make some larger sense of what had happened—and really we could not. We spent that week somewhat in a daze. It all seemed like a dream from which we would eventually wake.

I saw clearly the great void that opened in my parents' lives, bereft as they were of their last born. Sandra and I took our children and went back to Iowa, to the demands of graduate school and the challenges of rearing a young family. And our grief softened and soon lost its central place in our daily awareness. We had much else to think about. But that did not happen for my mother and my father. With passing months and years, I saw that such loss is different for parents than for others, including siblings. Parents have so much of themselves invested. Their offspring are their contribution to the future, an extension in some sense of themselves. The good lives of those offspring are the reward for the travail of bringing them forth, of bringing them up. Now, more than two decades later, I know this emotionally, from a parent's point of view. I understand now that my memories of Brad contain a core of grief that probably will never entirely fade.

Thinking of my parents and their loss, I have sometimes during the past three years wondered which is worse: To have, as with Paul, a loved one wrenched away from you suddenly by accidental death, as though stolen, with no warning, no preparation. Or to lose a loved one, as we did Brad, by stages, with ample time—too much time—to recognize and then become familiar with the inevitable drift toward death. To be an onlooker as a vigorous body and a quick mind are dismantled by degrees through the agency of a relentless virus, to watch as in the stricken one the desire for life ebbs and the longing for death grows. And to recognize with horror that you have come to share that longing for death's arrival. To experience vicariously the process that weans us from life's sweetness and reconciles us to its negation. In the aftermath, is that better or worse?

Clearly, in a case like the latter, one in which a loved one is terminally ill, much of the grieving is experienced before death comes. During Brad's last months, we reached decisive points at which we could not realistically hope for his recovery, points at which we could not avoid leavetaking and its attendant sorrow. In September when Ted departed to spend two years in Uruguay, the oldest and the youngest brothers embraced and said goodbye, knowing full well that they would not see each other again in this world. That farewell was a harbinger of death.

Another early watershed of grief was Brad's decision in mid-August to dispose of his valued possessions. The task was symbolic: it was a formal letting-go. There was an undeniable finality about that sorting through and considering who would value his books, his art objects. I did less well than Sandra in observing and talking with him about those decisions, for that process too was a little death.

Grief made another premature claim three weeks before the end when Brad decided to stop taking AZT, the experimental AIDS drug, and Bacterin, a powerful antibiotic. His decision was a considered acknowledgement that a quality recovery was no longer possible. If our sense of loss did not overwhelm us then, it was only because we were still preoccupied with the practical matters of seeing the illness through to the end. That was time- and energy-consuming, and to some extent it postponed the full payment of the emotional debt.

I have learned some things about how grief is shared, or often not shared. I have seen how compassion felt and expressed can bring enormous solace, but I have also realized how difficult it is for most of us to reach out more than superficially, or for the bereaved to invite such reaching out. As a result, there is, almost inevitably, a terrible isolation attending grief.

The isolation may be self-chosen. Some who suffer the loss of love, of reputation, of station, are like the wild duck in Ibsen's play. When wounded they plunge to the bottom of the lake and attach themselves to the weeds. Unwilling to confront their loss, or to encounter others who would remind them of it, such die a figurative death under water. But the majority of us who suffer grievous loss need to feel, I think, that the world has noticed and that the world cares. If this is so, why is it so hard to break through the barrier of isolation? Why, when we want so badly to express our puzzlement, our frustration, our woe to sympathetic ears, do such real encounters occur so infrequently? (I speak here of conversations that go beyond the well-meant but perfunctory expressions of sympathy: "We heard about your loss, and we are so sorry." "Thank you.")

There are a variety of reasons. To begin with, we who grieve are often too reluctant to broach the subject of loss. Perhaps we feel that to do so is to compel others to commiserate with us. At the most that seems presumptuous, at the least not sufficiently stoic. Ironically, others may interpret our seeming reluctance to mean that we do not wish to talk about our loss. They respect what they mistakenly believe to be communicated by our silence.

Sometimes kind acquaintances who would like to take the initiative simply lack the courage. They do not want to cause us pain, and they fear that bringing up the subject of our loss will be painful to us. Often they feel that they have not the words to articulate adequately, kindly and delicately, the consolation they would like to bring—so they remain silent. There are others—more than a few, I believe—who are themselves subconsciously troubled by the unpredictability of existence, by the threat of nihilism lurking in the shadows. Our problem is an unpleasant reminder of that which they would prefer to forget. And so they act as though life, ours as well as theirs, were proceeding calmly on an even keel.

Most troubling of all are those instances when the circumstances associated with one's loss are related to taboos, such as homosexuality or a disease like AIDS, taboos which arise from religious convictions, from simple prejudice, or from fear. When such conditions exist, the would-be comforter has difficulty dealing with the ambiguity of his feelings, or may despair of being able to express her honest sentiments without giving offense—and simply avoids the subject altogether.

Whatever the cause, I have been continually aware of people who knew of my loss and grief and probably would like to have reached out to comfort me—but couldn't, didn't know how to get across that abyss. (Sometimes it was I who could not bridge the gap, held back by pride, afraid I'd appear foolish if I expressed my feelings; on the other hand, a few times when friends indulged me, I have pinned them like Coleridge's wedding guest and unloosed upon them a flood of suppressed perplexity and outrage, until I recognized with some embarrassment my excess and their discomfort.) So many times I've been aware of pregnant opportunities when two persons could have talked about matters deeply important—when we could have spoken candidly of our humanity with all of its paradoxes and uncertainties—and those conversations died in embryo, impotent to be born.

But in another way, Sandra and I did get a more than usual number of opportunities to talk about our loss, including opportunities to speak with largely sympathetic groups. It was because AIDS was just then in 1987 much in the news, and awareness of its potential impact in the provinces was growing. So we were invited by church groups—Presbyterians, Episcopalians, Lutherans, Methodists (sadly, never by our own Mormon congregations)—to come and describe what our individual and family experience was like, isolated as we had been. We were invited by various health care providers and educators to explain in group settings how, without much support, we had fared in contending with a frightening set of circumstances. We always took advantage to say that our experience had to be seen in the context of societal and religious attitudes toward homosexuality.

Furthermore, I had written an article-length letter to one of our church's leaders, a letter in which I expressed much of what I felt in the weeks following Brad's death. Eventually, in altered form, that document began to circulate widely, generating a number of mostly friendly and sympathetic responses. It soon became known that we were willing to talk with people who were troubled by personal and familial experience with homosexuality or AIDS. Sandra especially became a kind of one-person, multifaceted support resource. She collected articles, books, pamphlets, tapes dealing with homosexuality and AIDS and became the center of a surprisingly active information service. We met and shared our experience with a good many people in varied contexts.

We undertook these activities partly out of love for Brad, as a way of belatedly trying to let the world know of our acceptance and support of him (which had not always been unconditional and obvious). Perhaps we hoped that in some mystical way he would know what we were doing. I think we believed it was a way of pursuing fairness and love in the world and of attempting to minimize the pain that many others feel. Undoubtedly we became involved to meliorate to some degree our pain. What we confronted in our loss was absurdity, and our activism was an instinctive, reflex effort to combat it. On the deepest level, we were satisfying our own psychological need.

Whatever the range of motivations, we were fortunate. We found opportunity to examine methodically our experience of loss, to sort through it with people who would listen, and thereby to alleviate the effects of grief stemming from isolation and silence. In this we have been more fortunate than many, who, grieving, have but limited opportunity to express their feelings, and who lack a purposeful cause to which they can redirect their emotions.

"We tell ourselves stories in order to live," writes Joan Didion at

the outset of *The White Album*. She is referring to a time when culture
and the events of her life seemed particularly devoid of coherence:

> We look for the sermon in the suicide, for the social or moral lesson
> in the murder of five. We interpret what we see, select the most
> workable of the multiple choices. We live entirely . . . by the
> imposition of a narrative line upon disparate images, by the "ideas"
> with which we have learned to freeze the shifting phantasmagoria
> which is our actual experience.

We are thus driven, Didion implies, because the human psyche
does not wish to confront ontological chaos. Existence must be
purposeful, its elements connected, and when we are confronted
with the prospect of absurdity, our minds go quickly to work
imposing patterns of meaning that have their real origins in ourselves. It is defensive action. Ingeniously—perhaps desperately—
we devise strategies rooted in myth, superstition, or other specious
correspondences to make existence bearable. Francis Bacon, that
severe empiricist, would accuse us of worshipping idols of the tribe,
the cave, and the theater. He would concur with Didion: "We tell
ourselves stories in order to live."

With more than a little conviction that they are right, I have seen
in myself during the past three years this very tendency, this
necessity to impose purposeful coherence in the absurd fabric of
my recent experience. Contemplating Brad's death, before and
after, my mind has pursued many an avenue, many a "what if," that
might hold the unthinkable at bay. I am not referring to large order
theological solutions, not for example the view that God willed
Brad's death, called him home, has another purpose for him just
now. That premise contains several problems for me. Rather, I refer
to much more modest evidence of coherence, small connections
that might be a sign, however indefinite, of hope.

Let me cite an example. We had a ficus fig tree in our living room
that we were fond of. In our previous dwelling it had flourished for
several years. But ficus figs are delicate. When we moved to 20th

Street the tree began to lose its leaves. No matter, before long it put out new light green ones. They grew to a little more than an inch in length, then they too fell. Before long new leaves appeared—only to abort after several weeks. The plant settled into a cycle, a series of leafings and unleafings, attempting gamely to rejuvenate itself. Sandra, who has a green thumb, ministered devotedly to the ficus, and I thought it would pull through.

Somehow that fig tree's fight for life became aligned for me with Brad's simultaneous struggle. I watched them both day by day, looking for any little indications of improvement, any signs of hope. If it could pull off a miracle and survive, so could he. It was not superstition exactly. I knew full well there was no material connection between the two. Yet I understand as a result of my preoccupation with this little tree how a troubled mind searches for correspondences, how it wants to invest the symbol with power. You focus your mental energy, your faith, on the object of your grave concern, and when that seems not enough to effect your desire you cast about to find some external help.

Oh, how I watched that tree. How I wanted it to recover. With each renewed effort it made to put forth leaves, I thought: "Surely, this is the beginning of its return to health."

Sandra tried this, she tried that—more light, less light, varied the watering, fertilized the soil, treated for insects. Gradually, with each new cycle there were fewer new leaves and fewer mature ones. I refused to acknowledge the decline, but several weeks before Brad died it was clear that the ficus was finished.

Another example. It was in late September, and I was feeling particularly burdened with grief. We had come to the point of planning for the end. On a Saturday afternoon I went out alone to hike on Haystack Mountain, just to get away for a few hours, just to get to where I could see the "big views." While I was up there on the mountainside, a thought came to me powerfully: I would tell Brad that after he died and passed over he should find Paul. The young uncle and his nephew, the first grandchild, had had a special fondness for each other. Paul had been dead for twenty years, he had been over there, he would know his way around. He could be a guide. For Brad to find him would be to find an immediate friend, a familiar haven. This ordinary thought, so predictable in a way, came to me with the force of an epiphany. It brought incredible comfort to me as I descended the mountain.

I must say here that the afterlife for which I hope is not something which normally I feel comfortable or confident imagining in particular detail. Agnosticism accompanies my existential faith. Knowing that Brad's view was somewhat like my own, I should have been prepared, I suppose, for his response to the "comforting advice" I offered on my return: he disparaged and abruptly dismissed it. One more reconciling story out the window.

Yet another modest example, the following summer, after Brad's death. Once again I was on Haystack Mountain alone. Descending from the summit, I rested for a short while in an aspen grove on the steep, shady north side of a ridge. Out in the azure, only a little above my eye level, two large hawks were riding the thermal updrafts, effortlessly circling, gliding, rising. It was lovely to watch. They stayed on and on. It came to me that somehow I was watching Brad. At the time of his death, Sandra had said, "He looks like an eagle, and now he is soaring beautifully." I remembered that image because I liked the connotations of a raptor's virility and freedom which seemed so appropriate to Brad's temperament.

Wasn't it somehow right that Brad would return to this mountain environment he loved? Wasn't it good to see him up there riding gracefully, so obviously at peace, in harmony with his elements? Wasn't it nice that he had found a companion with whom to share this hour? And hadn't he chosen this form and this time and this place to communicate to me from beyond death that he yet lives and thinks of us in the Idaho landscape where his mortal sensibilities were formed? I know this little experience was nothing more than poetic indulgence, an expression of my own deep longing, a small story I told myself in order to live through that particular period. But yes, it was comforting to me.

Dreams also must surely be included among the stories we tell

ourselves, although their genesis in the unconscious may sometimes make their intent less obvious. I am not a great dreamer, but
I have dreamed of Brad several times since his death with an
immediacy and vividness that were more overpoweringly real than
waking life. In one of those dreams, he returned to us like Lazarus
from death. To me in the dream this was wholly unexpected, it was
amazing. He was pale and thin, not merely from his mortal illness
but because death itself had been an ordeal. Yet he was smiling
gently and his countenance was radiant. Clearly, he was alive and
mending, and in the way of becoming transcendent. I believe the
reunion was as sweet to him as it was to me. I put my arms around
him, and I knew it was he, intact, tangible. At this point in the short
dream I felt a beatitude of such depth and joyousness as I think I
have never felt in life. I awoke shortly, but the afterglow lingered
through the morning.

What is one to make of such a dream? I dare not conclude that
it was an objective vision. It is too easily explained as subjective
wish fulfillment, the subconsciously created form in which my love
and longing found expression. But who can say for certain where
fantasy ends and reality begins. I do know that the feelings evoked
by the experience were sublime; it was as if I "on honeydew ha[d]
fed,/ And drunk the milk of Paradise."

I am struck by the similarities between the psychological stages
in the dying process as described by Elizabeth Kubler-Ross, including denial, anger, bargaining, despair, and acceptance, and the
progress of grieving that others experience. That the stages so nearly
correspond for the two groups is not surprising at all when one
recognizes that the dying person is, after all, so obviously a griever.
I want to comment here on the effects of anger as a part of that
process.

One of the ways the mind attempts to cope with inscrutable
deprivation is to find someone or something to blame. That at least
diminishes to a degree the absurdity by providing a cause-and-effect

explanation, and it provides an outlet for frustration. As I observed the extended suffering of my homosexual son, whom did I blame? Not Brad. Having already concluded that he was not responsible for his homosexuality, I considered him in his total experience more sinned against than sinning. He made mistakes, but he learned from them. Could I be angry at his mother and me? Ultimately not. Setting aside my earlier homophobia, we had tried hard to understand and assist him. We too had changed. Did I blame God? No. God's purposes are ultimately beyond my ken, and while I assume that they are benign, it would be foolish for me to presume to judge the infinite.

But did I blame our society for its close-mindedness and intolerance? Yes, I did, for those cultural attitudes were finite, very close to home, and there seemed to me little excuse for such callous indifference on the part of a self-declared religious nation toward the plight of persons like Brad. And did I feel anger toward some of those institutional pillars of Christianity which ought to have been in the forefront promoting tolerance, understanding, and a climate fostering individual self-realization? Yes, I did. For those institutions were immediately, conveniently at hand, and I thought their failures were stunning.

Our relationship with our own church was inescapably affected. We felt how ironic it was that the presumed haven of spiritual comfort for those distressed was to us, during our long period of perplexity, remote from what was happening in our lives. In the greatest extremity that any of us in the family had faced, our church simply was not there for us. How was this possible? The doctrinal position on homosexuality was only symptomatic of a larger problem concerning the church's epistemological view of how spiritual truth becomes known.

As the Mormons see it, prophets and others in the hierarchy are the conduits through whom God speaks. That means that on sensitive issues, real dialogue is pointedly discouraged. That means that in Latter-day Saint congregations there is no openness to discuss a matter such as homosexuality, except to dismiss it *a priori*.

Officially, the church shows little interest in examining or crediting experiential truth when it lies outside orthodoxy. Since our experience over the preceding seven years had led us to a contrary view of the causes and existential realities of homosexuality, an unspoken barrier rose between us and friends whose highest loyalty is to the authority of the church. Under these circumstances, how could we approach our brothers and sisters to share with them the incongruous division between doctrine and the actual experience with which we were struggling. We remained silent.

There were, to be sure, several of our Latter-day Saint friends who became aware toward the end of Brad's life of what was happening in our family. These included at least two of our ecclesiastical leaders, in whom we confided. On a personal level, these men responded with deep and sincere humanity. But they had no doctrinal comfort for us, nor could they speak out, then or now, to encourage through dialogue in their congregations a clearer, more tolerant understanding of homosexuality and its burdens.

For us, the implications of this situation extended beyond the issues relating to homosexuality. This experience simply added dramatic weight to our perception that organized religion is most concerned with conformity and preservation of the collective status quo. There would have been, I think, no lack of good will and support on the part of many of our LDS acquaintances if there had been a framework to encourage it. But the rigidity of the institutional church disarmed both their ability to respond helpfully and, not less important, our ability, even our willingness to allow them to do so. I remember two separate well-intentioned members of our ward who said to Sandra and me following Brad's death: "We want you to know that we don't think any the less of you because of what your son became." None of us felt sufficiently comfortable to pursue the ambiguity of those statements.

If I grieved during this period, some part of it was sadness that our spiritual community had been weighed and found wanting. In spite of my increasing unorthodoxy, the church had always been important to my identity. Now, with some regret, I saw it diminished, fading as a vital force in my life.

I have learned that remorse can profoundly influence grief. One of the heaviest burdens in the aftermath of loss is the nagging awareness that one might have done better by the departed loved one. Three years later I still find myself thinking that I was not all that I could have been to Brad in his ordeal. Why didn't I come out of the parent's closet while he was still alive and acknowledge openly to the world that I had a gay son of whom I am proud. Why did I accept the convenient path of avoidance by agreeing with him that it was prudent not to let the world know—or more precisely our generally narrow-minded community. Couldn't I by such an example have helped him know at a deeper level of my unconditional acceptance of him (was it really at that time unconditional?), and might that not have helped him leave this life with more personal acceptance and peace?

Moreover, did I really do all I could for him in terms of giving him my time? Should I, during his illness, have missed work more, should I have devoted less effort to finishing up the construction fo our house, less time to church-related activity? Should we have spent more money than we did to increase his comfort, to bring him a few additional pleasures. As we went through that last year, it seemed we did the best we could, yet now I wish I had done more. How much is enough? I know that this is not a rational response, but it is there nonetheless. I know that the worst of grief will not be over unless I can forgive myself for not having been more for him then.

———

DECEMBER 5, 1989, the third anniversary of Brad's death: a day fraught with melancholy. I am remembering that we did not spend his last mortal day entirely at his side. He had been hospitalized for six days. Sandra was with him during the morning. About noon

Brad told her he wanted to be quite alone. We understood. After all, we had been hovering about continuously. After work I stopped in to see how he was. Sleeping—quietly. I sat there in his room for half an hour, then went home. About nine thirty, I said, "Let's go to the hospital." When we got there we were startled to find him *in extremis*, struggling to breathe, sweating in agony. Why had the nurses not called us? We had needed to be there, if not for his sake at least for our own. We were terribly angry with them.

It was not an easy death. We are not sure to what extent he knew we were with him at the end. That haunts us. We were not able to tell him one last time—with assurance that he heard—that we love him, for somehow it seemed he was far away from us in the process of his dying, that we should not intrude too much in his solitude. And that haunts us. He was given a sedative about 11:00 on our request, and that probably hastened the end which came at 11:45. Did we do all that we could to support and ease his way in those last two hours. We do not know.

Where is he now, today? Has he found rest? On this day it is not easy to think of him as his old vital and intense self. I am too haunted by the memory of that gaunt face outlined sharply in a hospital bed. I remember too vividly his death throes. I pray he has had three years of peace and that he is happy, that he is among friends, that he feels our love reach out to him. But what if there is nothing beyond (this is not a natural thought to me, yet I must acknowledge its possibility)? Or worse (I contemplate this standing in my morning shower, trying to wake up): what if he is miserable, what if the state of the dead is a condition without shape or meaning, just frustrated, dark consciousness? I push this from my mind and pray with renewed fervor that he has found peace and is happy.

———

JUNE 1991. Many more months have passed. It is now six years since the recognized onset of Brad's illness, four and a half years since his death. According to conventional wisdom, time heals. That is partly true. While the months and years were passing, our wound of loss gradually scabbed over; little by little the crusty surface sloughed off, smoothed out. We have grown accustomed to his absence. To all outward seeming we go about our lives untroubled and well adjusted. We find pleasant days filled with challenging work, rewarding relationships, diverting experiences.

But to be accustomed is not necessarily to be reconciled. Time's healing is but partial. Under that apparently restored surface lies a small hard knot, an inflamed residue of pain, a concentrated core of grief that gnaws at psychic tranquility. I am convinced this will be a permanent dis-ease, Blake's invisible worm that lies concealed in the crimson joy of the rose.

Yet even if it could be dispelled by some deep healing, I think it should not be. I would be loathe to lose it altogether. It stands as a reminder of the truth about this flawed condition of mortality, a reminder—as Linda Loman tells Willy in Arthur Miller's *Death of a Salesman*—that "life is a casting off. It's always that way." I have acquired that knowledge dearly, and I do not wish to forget at what cost.

Epilogue:
The Great Western Cooperative

The Incarnation of Christianity implies a harmonious
solution of the problem of the relations
between the individual and the collective. . . .
This solution is precisely what men are thirsting for today.
—Simone Weil

A poor man inherited a small farm in another country. Overjoyed
at his good fortune, he journeyed there to take up his land and work
it for his living. When he arrived, he found his acreage located in a
well-developed agricultural region, surrounded by other small
holdings, each carefully cultivated by its owner. "Surely," he told
himself, "this bodes well. Clearly, the farmers on every side of me
are comfortable. Their lands and buildings are well tended. I am
sure that I too will prosper."

Early on the second day, a committee of neighbors came to call
on the newcomer. "Welcome in our midst," they said. "You see that
we are successful in our agricultural endeavors. It was not, we are
told, always thus in our region. We owe our present good fortune
to the establishment here of the Great Western Cooperative, a
wonderful organization that oversees all of our endeavors and
virtually guarantees that our farms and our lives will flourish. Since
you will doubtless also wish to be a member, we are here to tell you

that on Sunday next you may present yourself at the meeting of the Cooperative to be inducted."

And thus it happened that the man became a part of the Great Western Cooperative. "Surely," he reflected, "this bodes well."

Since he had not previously been a farmer and was only roughly acquainted with the methods of agricultural husbandry, he was grateful for his new friends and their Cooperative. Cheerfully, they advised him about crops and seasons, provided him with seed and fertilizer. They showed him how to use his implements, tutored him on the care of his animals, rented him machinery owned by the Cooperative. It seemed they had the answers for all his problems. "Best of all," they said, "when harvest time comes, the Cooperative will buy your crops and sell them. Our leaders know the markets, whereas you will doubtless take a frightful beating if you attempt to do your own marketing. It's a desperate world out there when you try to go it alone. Of course, the Cooperative takes a commission, but that is only as it should be, considering the benefits. In the meantime, just be sure you attend all the Cooperative meetings, on Sunday afternoons and on Wednesday evenings. That is where one learns what one needs to know about farming— irrigation and weed control and crop rotation, for example. And there we learn to take full advantage of the Cooperative."

"Well and good," said the man. He attended the meetings diligently, absorbed the instruction as best he could. And he worked hard in his fields. When fall came, his crops of corn and oats were good, and he sold them to the Cooperative. Moreover, because he had made good silage for his animals, he came through the long winter without hardship.

The second year began auspiciously. Spring came early, with good moisture, and the man prepared his land for planting. "I think," said he, "that this year I will raise barley, potatoes, and soybeans." But that Wednesday at the Cooperative meeting, the Section Leader informed him that, while barley and potatoes would be just fine, soybeans were not a possibility since the Cooperative did not favor soybeans and therefore did not stock soybean seed.

"Well, then I'll get my seed elsewhere," said the man. To which the Section Leader responded, "Members are expected to buy all their seed from the Cooperative. So, you see it really is not possible. Let us know when you want your barley and potato seed delivered. We can deliver your fertilizer at the same time."

"But," said the man, "I really won't need the Coop fertilizer this spring. You see, during the winter my cows produced a considerable hill of manure, and I plan to use that instead."

"I am sorry," said the Section Leader, "but all Cooperative members have to use the designated fertilizer. That's one of the conditions of membership."

"But what must I do with all of my manure?"

"No doubt," said the Section Leader, "you'll think of something." Then, under his breath he added: "The offensive thing about manure is that it's so earthy." This response troubled the farmer somewhat, but after all, he reflected, the Cooperative had proven greatly helpful to him thus far, and no doubt it was as his neighbors said: "The Cooperative directors know what is best for us."

Meanwhile, he continued to attend the Cooperative meetings faithfully, both Sunday and Wednesday. Truly, he did learn steadily about the methods of husbandry favored by the Westerners, though as time passed he began to feel that the returns on his attendance diminished. For one thing, it seemed that the Coop discussions rehearsed the same points again and again. So much repetition seemed both pointless and boring. On two occasions, as his own farming experience grew, he attempted to suggest innovative approaches to cattle breeding and irrigation of potatoes, only to be told that the correct methods had long been conclusively established; they were reviewed for members regularly, and he would do well to follow them without question. "Farmers who do not remain faithful to the accepted practices of the Cooperative inevitably drift into trouble," they said, "and in the long run cannot prosper."

But if the Cooperative followed a conservative approach to what might be called its theories about agriculture, it was, on the contrary, ambitious and innovative in its programs for aiding farm families. It proceeded from the assumption that farmers' lives are multifaceted, and that if one is to farm well, all of one's human needs must be satisfied. The Westerners were therefore organized to provide programs for everything from carpentry to square dancing, from farm-family relations to physical fitness. Part of the value of these programs, the Section Leader told our husbandman, lies in the fact that participation and association with right-thinking people are desirable. "One way to measure the health of the Cooperative," he said, "is to gauge the percentage of the members who participate in the recommended programs. Activity for everyone is our aim."

As usual, the Cooperative is right, thought the farmer; no doubt, I benefit. I have been a lonely man, and it is pleasant enough to join with my neighbors in games and social occasions. I am glad they care about me. But he noticed also that these activities required more of his time than simply Sunday afternoon and Wednesday evening. Sometimes he would have preferred to spend those additional evenings fishing in the creek that ran past his cottage or simply contemplating the setting sun from his rocking chair. But he felt some compulsion to join the others in the group activities, even when tired, for at Sunday afternoon meetings of the Cooperative each member was called on to account for his activities of the preceding week. One felt uncomfortable if he had not been "active."

The harvest came, and another winter. All the while, the manure pile behind the barn continued to grow.

One spring morning the Section Leader appeared at the barn door while the man was milking. "Will you come with me, brother, to visit your neighbor?" he asked. "We in the Cooperative are concerned about him." Such visits by representatives of the Cooperative were common, and the man agreed to accompany his leader.

They found the neighbor out in his field planting soybeans. "Good day, brother," said the Section Leader. "We come today out of concern for you. We have not seen you at Cooperative meetings for some time, nor have you participated in the optional programs.

We are surprised to find you here this morning planting soybeans—
and using a machine that clearly was not rented from the Cooperative. Can you tell us what lies behind this behavior?"

For a minute the neighboring farmer seemed embarrassed and
at a loss for words. But then he squared his shoulders, raised his
eyes and said: "If a man wants to raise soybeans, he should be able
to do it, if he is a man. It is he who should decide for himself."

"But," said the leader, "you know how the Cooperative feels
about soybeans; you know our directors will not buy and market
your crop, so you have no guarantees that your labor will be repaid.
If you misjudge the market, you will not have means to live through
next winter. Is that wise?"

"I will take that risk," replied the farmer. "If there is a chance that
I will fail, there is also a chance that I will do better than the Coop.
And now if you will excuse me, I must get back to work."

"Well, brother," said the Section Leader, "it's a dangerous path
you have embarked upon. I fear that you risk not only economic
loss but also loss of the good opinion of your friends. I fear you will
rue this."

The man left his neighbor's field and returned to his own farm
with unsettled feelings.

Week followed week, and as usual the man attended Cooperative meetings. But he began to feel a more pronounced dissatisfac-
tion with them. It was not merely that they were repetitious: he
gradually realized that the larger part of the time was spent not in
discussing farming methods but rather in discussing the Cooperative itself, how to make it work, how to keep all the Westerners
engaged and active in its programs, for, strange to say, more than
a few of them seemed prone to backsliding. Was it for this reason
that an inordinate amount of time was devoted to praising and
reaffirming the value of the Cooperative? Was this necessary to
make it seem indispensable to its members? Gradually, he began to
think of the Cooperative as being like a great machine, but not a
very efficient one, for it required an enormous amount of energy
and time, his included, simply to keep it in motion.

As the summer progressed, the man watched the soybean plants growing in his neighbor's field. They were diligently tended, they produced a fine yield, and the neighbor sold the crop directly to the processors at a favorable price. The man was pleased for his neighbor's good fortune; at the same time he felt oddly uncomfortable, for had not his neighbor defied the Cooperative?

That December when the man went to the Cooperative Center to give a summary of his farming practices for the year and an accounting of his financial returns as required by the Cooperative, he raised the matter with his Section Leader. "It was a good year for my neighbor's soybeans," he said. "I'm not sure how I feel about what he did, but I guess he was right, after all. I've been thinking that I'd like to plant soybeans next spring. Couldn't we talk to the directors and get them to approve soybeans for all the members?"

"Don't even think it," responded the Section Leader with some warmth. "Your neighbor was wrong to go against the policies of the Cooperative."

"But it seemed good to my neighbor to do what he did, and as a result he has provided well for himself and his family."

"He took a foolish risk," replied the Section Leader; "it is wise to be conservative and to follow good counsel. Even though he was lucky with the market, in the long run, he will not prosper, for our directors know what is best for us. Imagine what it would mean if everyone did as he did, if everyone simply chose to follow his own counsel and plant whatever he wished. Consider how the solidarity of the Cooperative would break down, how its marketing advantages would be lost. There is strength in our unity based on correct principles. Don't even think about soybeans. Your assignment for next year is to plant barley and corn. We'll deliver the seed in good time, along with the fertilizer you'll need. In the meantime, you're well advised to have as little as possible to do with your neighbor. Cultivate other friendships instead."

Throughout the winter, the man thought about his neighbor, he thought about soybeans, and he thought about the Cooperative. Meanwhile, his livestock turned good hay and silage into manure.

When spring came, the great accumulating mountain of it hid the entire end of the barn. "This situation does not make sense to me," thought the man; "Coop fertilizer will cost me money, and here I have all this manure. Why shouldn't I use it?"

Though he had some misgivings about doing so, he decided to ask his neighbor's advice. "Well," said the latter, "I understand your reasoning, and if it were me, I would spread the manure. But if you do, you must be prepared to be treated as I am treated. Some of my privileges within the Coop were withdrawn, and I am ostracized by all of my former friends. I no longer feel comfortable in having any connection with the Coop and have dropped out of it altogether. I suppose I prefer it that way, but being on the outside is lonely."

"Yes, I can see that," said the man. "Yet you are free—I have thought about it all through the winter, and I realize that you are free. I envy that. Frankly, I would like to plant soybeans, too."

"Think it over carefully," said the neighbor. "There is much good in the Cooperative. Many of its members are very pleased with it, for it is a supportive force in their lives and gives them exactly what they want. Remember how the Westerners helped you when you came. You knew so little about farming. Think how they taught you their proven methods. And think how they gave you a place among them, a chance to be part of their community. Think how they made your path smooth."

"That is true," said the man, "and I acknowledge it. In some ways I don't want to lose those things. Perhaps I won't lose them, after all, even though I think I must spread that manure and plant my ground in soybeans."

Well, within a few days the end of the man's barn had again come into view, and a load of soybean seed in an unfamiliar wagon was delivered to his farm.

It was only a matter of days before all the farmers in the vicinity knew of the man's defiant actions. Nevertheless, he attended his section meetings, determined that he would make a case for soybeans, persuaded that his friends would listen with open minds, would understand and approve. But he found they were uncomfortable even talking about such independent initiatives, and as the weeks passed he dropped the subject entirely. Gradually he sensed that fewer and fewer of them greeted him at section meetings, and then they did so only when they could not avoid it. He became aware of a widening gulf between himself and the others in the group.

It became easier for him to justify evenings spent fishing on his creek or simply reading in his rocking chair, and he gave up participation in Coop games and socials. He felt ambivalent about these changes. There was satisfaction in knowing that he now had time to do some things he really wished to do, and he was glad to have achieved some greater measure of self-determination. Yet at the same time he occasionally did miss the dancing and the games, and he grieved a little that he could not have the good fellowship he had previously enjoyed. Perhaps he even felt a little guilty about his desertion. The joy of his new sense of freedom was undercut somewhat by his realization that the Cooperative connection was moving beyond his choice. What he really wanted was to have the possibility of some of the Cooperative advantages without having to be totally confined within its limits. He found, to his sorrow, that he could not have it both ways. Late that summer he ceased attending meetings altogether.

The feeling of estrangement grew. It was not that his old Cooperative friends were hostile; it was just that they felt uncomfortable with him since he had adopted a qualified view of their world. As a result, the man sometimes found his lot difficult. If his machinery broke, he had no one to turn to for assistance, or at least his pride prevented him from it. When his livestock were ill, and his own knowledge was insufficient to treat the problem, some of his cattle died. Under the circumstances, how could he bring himself to appeal to the Coop and its resources. It is true that his soybean growing neighbor did attempt to assist him on occasion, especially with advice about the cultivation of soybeans, but the neighbor was by nature a rather private person, and so that relationship had its limits also.

That fall the man harvested only a mediocre crop of soybeans, and the market price had fallen more than a little relative to the previous year. Meanwhile, Cooperative farmers got good prices for barley, oats, corn, and potatoes. The man could not help questioning himself at that point. "Perhaps, after all, the Coop leaders do know what is best. Had I followed their advice, I'd have made twice the profit from my crop. As it is, I will only just manage to survive until next year." But after some time had passed and his discouragement wore off a little, he realized that, had he to do it again, he would still plant soybeans. "I am a man," he thought, "and there is a good deal more to farming than just making a profit."

Two more years went by. The man experimented with other crops, as it seemed good to him, and he marketed them himself. With some it went well enough, with others badly. However, he managed to get by. Gradually, his former acquaintances showed some renewed interest toward him, which took the form of periodic invitations to renew his affiliation with the Cooperative, to give up his idiosyncratic farming, and to follow again the programs of the Cooperative. To which he would customarily reply: "Thank you, your invitation is appealing. But I think I must go on farming after my own inclinations."

A year later the man offered his small farm for sale. "Where are you going, and why are you leaving?" asked his soybean-growing neighbor. "Can't you make a living?"

"Oh yes," he replied, "I do well enough to live. Like you, I am learning to be free, and that compensates for any material thing I might want. But I have decided to return to my old country."

"Have the soybean haters driven you out?" asked the neighbor.

"Not exactly," replied the man. "It is true that I'm a little lonely now, but I don't feel much overt hostility here. Ultimately, no one prevents me from working my land as I choose. I've been able to establish my independence, as you have done. Perhaps there are even some among the Westerners who give me a degree of qualified respect.

"But finally it seems I cannot breathe easily in this environment.

I was not cut out to live among Westerners. I learned a lot from them about farming, and, strange to say, without intending to they taught me much about myself. Now I know that as long as I remain in this land there will always be an incompatibility between them and me. A benign incompatibility, perhaps. But I cannot easily breathe this utopian air.

"So I am returning to my old country. With some luck, I'll buy a small farm there and try to raise soybeans. The climate there is cool and the growing season is short, but I'm of a mind to try raising cantaloupes and possibly some oranges, too."